The GIFT is in the PAIN

*One Woman's Journey
from Shackles to Freedom in Christ*

BY GEORGETTE CRANDALL FOSTER

Dedications

This is for you, Xaria, my beautiful daughter:
You were just a child when you were caught
in the web of my sin. I'm so sorry!
I love you endlessly.

To my mother Delores:
You are the best mom and grandmother.
Thank you.

To my cousin Novlette:
You rode the roller coaster of my life with me.
Thank you.

Table of Contents

Meet a woman who truly sought God but on her own terms rather than His. Her pursuit led her on a winding path of poor choices, a bittersweet relationship which bound her in chains, and much time spent out of God's will. However, God, in His mercy, was faithful in pursuing her all the while. He ultimately had to bring about a major catastrophe in her life to bring her to her knees and cause her to cry out to Him for redemption.

Georgette Crandall Foster, born in Jamaica, immigrated to the United States over 20 years ago. She is happily married to Clive Foster. She brought four beautiful children to the marriage: Xaria, 20, Dante, 13, and twins, Jayden and Jayda, 10. Living in the Orlando, Florida, area, she works in the insurance industry.

A multitalented lady, Georgette has written the lyrics to two complete CDs of worship and praise to her Redeemer sung by guest artists. She and her husband also have a Facebook program entitled, "Let's Talk with Clive and Georgette."

She has prayerfully written this book to help others avoid the many mistakes she has made in her life by sharing not just the profound heartaches she and her children experienced, but more importantly, to give hope to others who find themselves in circumstances out of which they do not believe they can escape. Jesus stands at the ready to rescue each and every person from their sin, no matter how great. "Behold, I stand at the door and knock; if anyone hears My voice and opens the door, I will come in to him and will dine with him, and he with Me" (Revelation 3:20).

On a personal note, Georgette and I were in a Bible Study Fellowship International class together. I admired her sweet spirit and desire to learn more about the Christ who had saved her. I was very much drawn to Georgette, but we never exchanged more than the usual pleasantries.

One day, toward the end of class, she approached me to consider editing this book you hold in your hands. She thought I had been an English teacher, but rather it was Spanish and French I had taught. I believed myself capable of such a task and offered to edit a portion for her to judge my abilities. As they say, the rest is history.

It has been my great joy and privilege to immerse myself in Georgette's story and work to make it an approachable, honest, and nail-biting journey through her young life to date. She has much to share with others from her personal experiences—not just with women, but also with men. I pray this recounting of her life so far helps many people avoid some of the pitfalls into which Georgette fell and helps others to escape before sinking so deeply. Thank you, Georgette, for sharing your inspiring story.

Dawne Stanton Nock
Editor, friend
October 2018

Author's Preface

What a journey writing this book has been! While a time-consuming project, my loving husband has unfailingly supported me every step of the way. How thankful I am to be the wife of such an awesome, patient, and caring man. Clive, you complete my life in every way. Thank you, for being a committed husband and father. The role you took on as my husband and the father of my children, has been done with grace, compassion, and love.

I survived my many years in the wilderness on the strength of my family, on the patience and unconditional love I received from them. Xaria, my oldest, lived through the most excruciating twists and turns, yet came through it all as a compassionate, loving young woman. Dante, I will always love you—God rescued you for His glory. Jayden and Jayda, God doubled my blessings when He gave me both of you in one bundle of joy as twins. As my life has unfolded, you all traveled on the journey with me. Through all the trials, poor choices, and mistakes, we have remained a close knit, devoted family.

To my mother, Delores, you complete the puzzle of our lives. You accepted the burdens of raising my children—your grandchildren. You took care of our home and were the glue which held our lives together. Most of all, you rode on my roller coaster of emotions without complaining. You, Mama, carried me, when I was too broken to carry myself.

Patrice, thank you for the time you invested in this book. Often, I wanted to quit, but you continued to speak love and patience into my life, encouraging me to continue. You weren't just a ghostwriter, you are family to me. Thank you.

Dawne, you nailed it. When I came to you, all I wanted you to do was read through this book because I thought all that was needed to complete the project was a second pair of eyes. How wrong I discovered I was when you started sending me the corrections and changes. In committing yourself to editing this book, you were tenacious about keeping us both on track in meeting our deadlines. Your husband jumped in and listened as you read aloud while on your long journey by car. As if that weren't enough, along came your son with his computer knowledge, helping with the more technical aspects.

You are an amazing person, Dawne. I did not choose you to edit this book, God did, and I'm truly grateful. I thank you and your family from the depths of my heart. I will always be grateful for the bond God has created between us. Thank you for allowing me to disagree with an opinion you had about a statement or two. Thank you for not changing my story as some editors would do. Thank you, Dawne, for your beautiful family that now has also become mine.

Ultimately, I want to give all the glory to my Lord Jesus for bringing me through the fiery trials of my own design, preserving my children and me as a close, loving family, and for lifting me up as on eagle's wings to serve Him as He desires (Exodus 19:4-6; Isaiah 40:31).

Georgette Crandall Foster
October 2018

Psalm 107:17-22

Fools, because of their rebellious way,
And because of their iniquities, were afflicted.

Their soul abhorred all kinds of food,
And they drew near to the gates of death.

Then they cried out to the Lord in their trouble;
He saved them out of their distresses.

He sent His word and healed them,
And delivered them from their destructions.

Let them give thanks to the Lord for His lovingkindness,
And for His wonders to the sons of men!

Let them also offer sacrifices of thanksgiving,
And tell of His works with joyful singing.

CHAPTER 1

The Opportunity of a Lifetime

Coming to America is a dream come true. Life here is very different from the one I had known in Jamaica. The United States is a whole new world to me; I think it is fantastic. I see and experience things that I had only seen on television. And I love every moment of the opportunity laid out in front of me, like a fine meal laid out at a lavish banquet.

The simplest of things are like heaven on earth, and I take nothing for granted. I have never seen people of so many different nationalities and languages. Our motto in Jamaica is "Out of Many One People." Yet the nationalities represented by the people of United States far surpass those in Jamaica.

While I was experiencing life to the full, the best for me was just an exciting view of the opportunities that lay ahead. At that point in time, I believed I had not achieved much, but my dreams and hopes were so vivid that I could feel them about to burst to fruition.

I came to this country with a determination to have a better life and to achieve my dreams. As I reflect on my own life, I experienced a humble beginning. In Jamaica, a balanced meal was a rarity. Frankly, my mother made dinner from whatever was available. Most of our meals came from buying on credit a little bit of cooking oil and some flour from the corner shop. Lemonade was the only affordable drink and sometimes it was served without ice.

My first job in the United States was working nights in a prominent restaurant, cleaning toilets. I saw scrubbing toilets as beneath me, and I became very scornful. In fact, I wasted a lot of time murmuring and complaining, even though I wore thick gloves to protect my hands. Being scornful did not get me anywhere. In fact, it took much longer to complete the job as I incessantly grumbled.

If you do your job joyfully, you will complete it more quickly, but if you do it disdainfully, it will take you forever. It's amazing what changing your mindset will do for you. If you can find contentment in all situations, you can find joy, peace, and love (Philippians 4:11-13).

There was a time in my life when my bed was a blue towel.

†

There was a time in my life when my bed was a blue towel. I would spread my towel out on the floor in my cousin's living room every night. Yes, it was inconvenient and uncomfortable; at times I tossed and turned, but once I fell asleep, it was sweet dreams. God has a way of providing for us no matter how meagre and uncomfortable the circumstances of life. There are seasons of life that He allows us to go through, and it's for us to accept them. I will always be grateful to my cousin who gave sacrificially for me.

What I learned from my past experiences gave me compassion for people who are going through similar situations today. Don't you have to start somewhere in life? God can start you from anywhere He desires. Some of you will never be able to grasp what God is doing in your life because of the way He chooses to start you on your journey to His blessings.

Sometimes God wants you to experience the lows of life and rise above them. The low points teach you compassion, humility, and love when you have nothing. As you grow and mature in Christ, you are humbled and learn to share in the pain of others. When you have picked up your cross and followed Christ, you have made up your mind that you are going to share in His persecution. Your anthem will be for God I live, for God I die, blessed be the name of the Lord.

Graditude helps you count your blessings.

†

One's peace comes by having confidence in Him. Even though I was working still, I didn't have the security for which I was looking, but I was very grateful for all the opportunities God was giving me. Gratitude helps you count your blessings.

CHAPTER 2

A Tangled Web

I had a mighty determination to achieve more than my childhood had offered in terms of material goods. Determination is a good tool to catapult you into achieving the purpose God has for your life, but can be treacherous when applied with covetousness. You can be determined, but don't be anxious or you will quickly accept the devil's proposition.

I was introduced to someone who needed a secretary at a mortgage company. This led me to working two jobs. I cleaned early mornings and then worked at the mortgage company during the day. It was difficult because I cleaned from midnight until five in the morning then rushed to get ready for work and make the bus to the office. I was constantly tired, but I needed both incomes to support myself and my daughter. Thank the Lord my mother had graciously taken Xaria to Jamaica with her for an extended period of time, so I could manage working two jobs.

At the mortgage company, one of the brokers resigned; I was trained for the position and was able to get my mortgage broker's license. While attending class, I met a very nice anglo guy, Matt, who imparted wisdom that I use even now. He told me that when I go to work, be sure to learn and understand three new things every day, then, at the end of the month, I will have learned ninety things about the business. I took that advice and continue to use it every day and encourage others to do the same.

I met Rob at my day job as a mortgage broker through a co-worker. He was handsome, well-groomed, and well-liked, and seemingly financially secure. He was close friends with my boss and visited the office quite often.

One day he was at the office until closing, and he asked if he could give me a ride home—I said yes. We exchanged phone numbers and started to communicate with each other on a regular basis. In no time, he picked me up every day after work whenever he was in town.

Our relationship blossomed with the help of a friend. I fell for Rob hook, line, and sinker. After spending some time with him, I decided he was mine for the keep. He changed my living situation in an instant. Rob taught me how to drive and then bought me a car. Soon thereafter, we were living together in an apartment he rented.

I never questioned him about his life or his family; frankly, I did not want to know about them. Shortly afterward, he moved me from a rental apartment to our own house. I watched my daughter as she slept in her own bed, in her own room. How generous was that? I thought over and over in my mind, *I must be dreaming.*

When I met Rob, I was involved with Mitch. He and I shared a daughter together and were planning to marry, but he was living elsewhere at the time. Rob took my breath away and I zoomed in on his ability to fulfill my childhood dreams. I remember how much pain Mitch felt when I told him our relationship was over. I have never seen a man cry so hard and beg me not to leave, but Rob had everything I thought I wanted. Mitch did not have the financial stability for which I was looking.

Zechariah 4:10 encourages us to not despise these small beginnings. But during that time, I was not focused on biblical principles; only what I wanted mattered. When you get a taste of Satan's proposal, he'll put blinders on your eyes so that you see only what he has to offer. And just as surely, I desired much of what the world had for me. Living in the United States was a bit like moving to Disneyland.

Rob recognized my knowledge of the mortgage industry, therefore he started a mortgage brokerage company. I was the brains of the business and he was the security for which I longed. He provided exactly what I wanted for me and my daughter. I became an investment for Rob and our relationship quickly became a win-win for both of us.

One thing about me, I'm not a timid person. I'm definitely a go-getter. Financially, we were doing well. I became established in the community of southeastern Florida through a local radio talk show. It was a fifteen-minute show about the mortgage business that I continued for a time. My name became a household staple for the listeners of this radio station. People could identify me by the sound of my voice or the mention of my name.

My most rewarding moment at work was sitting with each client and building a relationship with him or her. My friends would say I was a good salesperson. I could sell sand at the beach and people would happily buy it.

I felt like I was the only available woman on planet Earth when with Rob. He took me to the finest restaurants and on extravagant shopping sprees. I would try on the clothes he chose for me and swirl in them to get his approval. It was an amazing feeling as he gave me the thumbs up or thumbs down. Everything seemed perfect!

My childhood dreams were being fulfilled and my daughter Xaria was experiencing them with me. He was generous in everything concerning me. I turned a blind eye to the things I did not want to see. How many women do the same thing to keep their lives intact? Some may say they don't want to "rock the boat." I wanted to enjoy my new life for as long as I could.

I learned to ignore the undesirable things about Rob that were blatantly obvious to everyone else. I was so far gone, consumed with my own wishful thinking, that I chose to ignore the voice of reason. That was the wrong decision and I soon found out just how devastating a turn my life was going to take.

One day at the office, the first of a series of troublesome events occurred. As I was speaking with a male customer on the phone, Rob became extremely angry. He was loud and obnoxious, with no regard that the person on the other line could hear him. When I saw the infuriating look on his face, I quickly finished my phone call.

I was puzzled, because I had never seen him like that before. Seeing that side of him made me want to leave the office immediately. As I picked up my purse and walked out of the office, he met me at the door. He shoved me so hard that I staggered backwards and finally landed on my backside in the parking lot several feet away from him.

I sat where I fell for a few minutes with my face covered by my hands, and in the hot sun, wept in disbelief. At that moment, my life changed, and I started to unpack the contents of the package I had purchased. I picked myself up and started walking to nowhere sobbing with every step I took.

When you fall into the snare of the enemy, it's very difficult to extricate yourself. Imagine a trap set for an animal.

The bait is attractive and accessible, but once the animal is drawn in, escape is nearly impossible.

I was living my life trapped in a snare.

†

That's exactly how I was living my life—trapped in a snare. Rob drove up beside me, apologizing for his actions. He convinced me to get into the car with him. Yes, eventually and reluctantly, I relented. I sobbed in disbelief; I was totally confused and didn't know what to do or how to do it. How was I to escape to the unknown? I realized I was trapped in a very tumultuous relationship with seemingly nowhere to turn.

I faced verbal and physical abuse from Rob during our relationship. He was the only man to ever lay hands on me, not once, not twice … I lost count.

I endured the depths of emotional and physical pain, a secret I kept from everyone. What have I done? I asked myself. I had made a huge mistake, but I felt like I was drowning in the deep end with no one to rescue me. The memories of my relationship with Mitch and how much he loved and respected me were haunting. What seemed like not enough at the time became the desire and longing of my soul. I wanted Mitch's love back, but I couldn't have it because he had already moved on with his life.

Sometimes happy memories hurt when you're living in pain and sorrow. It took the remembrance of that hurt for me to tell you that relationships are not about money and material gain. God "is able to do exceedingly abundantly beyond all that we ask or think, according to the power that works within us" to His glory, not our own (Ephesians 3:20-21). The abundance He gives us is the deep joy we find in having an intimate relationship with Christ and living for Him in accordance to His will.

When I met Rob, he was already involved with another woman. I did not push him to break off the relationship, because Rob had not kept her a secret, and in fact gave me the distinct impression that the relationship was near terminating because of issues he was having with her. The more he told me of her, the more I believed the relationship would soon be over. Besides, I didn't want to make waves; I wanted to enjoy the security he offered me and my daughter.

What I did not foresee was that once I began my relationship with him, it would not be easy for me to break it off. I wanted nothing to do with my foolish choice of being the other woman, of getting involved before he was single, yet I ended up staying way longer than I wanted. When you are led by Satan, your own flesh, and the world, wrong feels right and right feels wrong; life will always be about you and no one else. Isaiah 5:20 makes this clear, "Woe to those who call evil good, and good evil; who substitute darkness for light and light for darkness; who substitute bitter for sweet and sweet for bitter!"

I had succumbed to the enticements of this world.

†

The other woman found out about me, and soon she called me constantly with raucous threats. I could not feel her pain until I experienced it firsthand. After dealing with the abuse for some time, I wanted Rob to leave me. I understand this woman was angry with me. If only she knew how much I wanted her to keep him because I no longer wanted him.

I realized the other woman was not the problem as Rob had stated, but that <u>he</u> was the problem. After a while Rob and his children's mother broke up and I thought it was just us, but I was in for a surprise. I would learn later that there was a third woman with children in our crowded and tangled web. What you sow you shall also reap (Galatians 6:7-8). I had succumbed to the enticements of this world.

I had forgotten the Word of God which says, "seek first His kingdom and His righteousness, and all these things will be added to you" (Matthew 6:33). Walking out of the will of God took me on a downward spiral. I found myself in a David and Bathsheba saga except murder was not a part of our story (2 Samuel 11).

Rob was very authoritative, and as long as I moved at his command all was well. I had to make sure everything was the way he wanted. I was diligent about this for Xaria's sake as I knew she was afraid of Rob and trembled at his very presence. When I cried, she cried. Far too often, she witnessed my abuse and consequently hers.

Many times, her little arms wrapped around my leg in search of comfort from Rob's wrath. There were days after the abuse that I held her and sobbed. What had I done? My lust for worldly gain, and therefore my decision to stay with Rob, had caused her much pain and distress, and I was in no shape to change our circumstances. I always warned her never to tell anyone about the abuse.

As if dealing with Rob wasn't enough, issues with past girlfriends emerged. I was one person up against his past—and present—girlfriends and the children they shared with Rob. My fairytale world had become a reality of hell, and attacks came from every angle. Even though his former girlfriends didn't like each other, with the intentions of destroying me, they came together in a united front to bring me down.

But lay up for yourselves treasures in heaven, where neither moth nor rust destroys, and where thieves do not break in or steal; for where your treasure is, there your heart will be also.

Jesus, Matthew 6:20-21

CHAPTER 3

Generosity Doesn't Always Mean Love

I quickly learned generosity doesn't always mean love. Many women, and even men, base their relationships on what the other party has to offer financially. Giving without sacrifice in a relationship isn't love, and I don't believe it is from God.

Gifts mean more when they come through sacrifice and from the heart. Unfortunately, some people give gifts generously to try and convince you they love you. It's actually a self-serving ploy to get what they want.

Men and women like to entice each other with expensive gifts, especially while dating. It feels good at first, but in most instances, it's temporary. It's but a gambit to lure the desired individual into their grasp. Today, many women are walking the path that I have walked.

These women have an imaginative description of the man they want to be their spouse. Dating or marrying someone for any other reason than love sets the stage for unforeseen, negative issues. I talk about this because, as reluctant as I am to admit it, that's just what I did. Now my life belongs to God, the Provider of my life, and because the Lord has sent someone to be my husband, regardless his status, I have gladly accepted him as a gift from God. It doesn't matter about his geographical background, his educational, or material achievements. There are more blessings when a man and woman are blessed by God and joined together as one.

I encourage you to trust God and receive the gift He has sent your way. He knows the beginning and the end, which means He also knows the in between of every situation. He may choose a man or woman to be your husband or wife because there may be circumstances you will face sometime in your future.

That individual is going to stand with and love you when you need this most. If you are sick, he will be there—whether happy or sad. Doesn't that mean more to you than generosity without love? I spent many nights alone whether I was sick or well, happy or sad, all in the name of financial gain.

It is more generous to have your spouse with you through thick and thin, through sickness and health. Taking your marital vows seriously is the greatest love and security spouses give one another. When God is in the choosing, the provisions have already been made. You may have a house, a car, money in the bank, and a successful business, along with everything that comes with these things, except a husband or wife with whom to share your life, should God choose to provide.

Now you realize something is missing and here comes a man or woman with nothing but love, which is the missing piece of your puzzle. Will you be able to share all your possessions in return for his or her true love to complete the puzzle?

God provided for you, not so you can hoard what He has given, but so you will share it. Whenever God blesses you, you should be a blessing to others. Remember, you can achieve material things through love, but you will never achieve love through material things.

> *Remember you can achieve material things through love, but you will never achieve love through material things.*

†

What does your checklist look like for your soul mate? I wanted a man who could provide for me to live the dreams of my childhood such as a house, car, nice clothes, fine restaurants, and more. This came with a price, a very costly price. My experience with Rob gave me a different view of life.

He provided for me and my daughter after we moved to the United States with nothing. I thought our relationship was on a great path; he gave me what I missed from my childhood and it brought me temporal happiness.

I also encountered what became the worst aspects of my new life—loneliness, sleepless nights, and many years of heartache. I had no idea what was in store for me as the relationship progressed, and I believed I had nowhere to turn.

Let me encourage you to love for love's sake because God is love. Do not compromise with the enemy. Wait on God!

You will not be afraid of the terror by night, or of the arrow that flies by day; of the pestilence that stalks in darkness, or of the destruction that lays waste at noon ... For you have made the Lord, my refuge, even the Most High, your dwelling place. No evil will befall you, nor will any plague come near your tent.

Psalm 91:5-6, 9-10

CHAPTER 4

My Roots

As for my humble beginnings, I am the fifth child of seven children, five boys and two girls. My older sister had immigrated to England when I was quite young, so in my early teens I quickly learned how to cook, clean, and wash clothes—all by hand.

My father worked in the sugar cane fields daily while my mother took care of the home and prepared meals for the family. In those days, a balanced meal was rare.

My mother has the heart of a lioness.

†

When the household funds were low, my mother joined my father in the sugar cane fields. Day after day, in the hot sun, she scattered fertilizer and picked up the leftover burnt cane that the tractor had left behind. It was difficult for me to accept both parents working so hard, but more so my mother. That was certainly not a job for a woman, but nothing could stop her. My mother has the heart of a lioness. She kept food on the table no matter how small the portions were; dinner was often made from whatever was available. When she worked in the fields her schedule demanded that she leave home early in the morning and return late at night.

There were days when she did not go to work because of the rainy weather. I would be so happy to have her home with us. Both of my parents worked very hard struggling to support their family.

My childhood memories take me back to bathing outside in a large metal tub, cooking dinner out-of-doors on a wood fire, and scrubbing the floors, down on my knees, with a little brush made of coconut husk. All of this was part of the normal life in our community.

Just getting to school was another challenge since there were no assigned school buses. I had to walk several miles to get a "taxi," a van that picks up various riders along their route. I then had to walk another couple of miles more after getting out of the taxi to get to school on time. Many taxi drivers were afraid to come to our neighborhood because it was an impoverished, rural area with old, broken down fences and houses. The roads were quite inaccessible and the people who lived there were thought to be dangerous. All of this conspired to make relying on these taxis problematic.

Children as young as seven years old knew how to cross the busiest road and how to get to school walking along those busy roads. Rain or shine you had to get to and from school on your own. I learned so much living in rural Jamaica. Do I appreciate it looking back? Of course, it was the best part of my life. It taught me compassion for the less fortunate and helps me now to be more readily available to be used by God, especially in helping folks who need a hand up. I want others to experience the same blessings I have had in creating a better life for myself and for my family.

Five of us shared the one children's bedroom available, so having the privacy of my own bedroom was not within the realm of possibility. Nevertheless, I found it to be fun because I had my brothers with me all the time. That was the way of life for us and many other families. However, when I got a glimpse of the upper-class communities, my desire for what they had increased my hope and wonder. I thought, would my Cinderella-like wishes ever come true?

I don't believe I would be who I am today, if I could have chosen where I was to be born. As a child, I wished I had been born into a different family, one that was financially stable and able to give me a better life. However, being born in impoverished, rural Jamaica didn't determine my full potential or success, nor do your difficult circumstances need to determine yours.

Most Christians are familiar with the following well-known question: After being called by Jesus, Philip testified to Nathanael, "We have found Him of whom Moses in the Law and also the prophets wrote—Jesus of Nazareth, the son of Joseph" (John 1:45). Nathanael replied with the question, "Can any good thing come out of Nazareth" (v. 46)? Many ask the same question today, "Can anything good come out of dire poverty?" Here I am, along with many others, who, by the grace of God, have risen above our circumstances. I can attest to the fact that God can use anyone despite his geographical location or family history.

It seemed easier to accept life as it was at home with my family simply because it was our reality. My grandfather had built our five-bedroom home with cement blocks, which was unusual in our community. It stood out and was, in many ways, a facelift for the area. Homes are more typically built of found wood and are much smaller.

My grandfather's three children were part of this inheritance, and therefore not only did my Mom live there with her family but her two siblings and their families also. The home was well occupied with cousins, uncles, and girlfriends. Even though one of my uncles, my Mom's brother, bought a house and moved out with his family, the home was overflowing with people, all of whom had the right to live there. It would have been improper to even suggest we make other arrangements. This was quite an inconvenience, to say the least.

A lot happened in the community and nothing remained hidden. Your life was an open book. The community was small, and everyone knew each other very well; therefore, news got around quickly.

Living in this rural area was very challenging and not everyone had an opportunity to have a better life. As I grew older and was reaching puberty, I was molested by the people closest to me. I experienced hugs that were a little bit too tight and was even touched in highly inappropriate ways.

This was horrifying yet I was too afraid to let my parents know. I thought it would create a public scene or that no one would believe me. Either way, I was afraid to tell anyone about it, so I kept it to myself. I was approximately ten years old at the time—how was I going to stand up to those men? I felt I couldn't, so I dealt with it by being fearful of men in general and keeping my distance.

Every day I encountered men whom I should have been able to trust as a young child. Being in the presence of those men made me very uncomfortable, and I truly wished I never had had to be in their presence at all. The simplest conversations with them were very unnerving. As a child, I was afraid, but as an adult, I felt unclean.

Now, as a mother, I find myself being very protective of my children. I am vigilant about where they sleep and who sleeps over. As parents, we must be very discerning. Most of those men who molested me were highly respected and pretended to be playful. All parents need to be very careful of their children sitting in laps and being held by "playful" adults. Speaking with other women, I've learned that I am not alone.

For many years, my experiences made me very anxious until I matured more in Christ. Greater maturity has taught me forgiveness, regardless of the hurt. My memories aren't as painful as they used to be. I thank God for His healing touch and for getting me through the worst of the difficult recollections. As a matter of a fact, I rarely think about them anymore. Praise the Lord! "Be anxious for nothing, but in everything by prayer and supplication with thanksgiving let your requests be made known to God. And the peace of God, which surpasses all comprehension, will guard your hearts and your minds in Christ Jesus" (Philippians 4:6-7).

Sometimes I wonder if those men now recognize that what they did was wrong, was sinful. Still to this day, when I return to Jamaica for visits and see any of them, I feel sick to my stomach and somewhat unclean.

I have forgiven the individuals who have trespassed against me, and I hope they have truly repented and have asked God for forgiveness. I learned quickly that spiritual maturity begets forgiveness. Matthew 18:21-35 tells the following story, "Peter came and said to Him, 'Lord, how often shall my brother sin against me and I forgive him? Up to seven times?' Jesus said to him, 'I do not say to you, up to seven times, but up to seventy times seven.'"

Jesus then goes on to relate the Parable of the Unmerciful Servant whereby He illustrates the kingdom of heaven: A king forgave the enormous debt of one of his slaves and that slave turned around and refused to forgive the debt of a fellow slave and threw him into prison. The remaining slaves were very grieved and went to their lord, the king, and told him all that had happened. The king summoned the forgiven slave, admonished him, and turned him over for punishment until he could repay [author's paraphrase]. Jesus ends the parable with these words, "So shall my heavenly Father also do to you, if each of you does not forgive his brother from your heart."

A strong illustration of forgiveness indeed.

I know God has now cleansed me from all uncleanliness along with the guilt I carried for years. Even though I was not responsible for the molestation I experienced as a child, I felt condemned at times. Condemnation is from our adversary, Satan, who is the father of all lies (John 8:44).

Satan and his minions know how to remind us of our past and the guilt we carry.

†

Satan and his minions know how to remind us of our past and the guilt we carry. They hit right where it hurts the most and when you least expect it. Thank God there is no condemnation for those who are in Christ Jesus (Romans 8:1). "If we say that we have fellowship with Him and yet walk in the darkness, we lie and do not practice the truth; but if we walk in the Light as He Himself is in the Light, we have fellowship with one another, and the blood of Jesus His Son cleanses us from all sin" (1 John 1:6-7).

Forgiveness is for everyone—the victim who needs to forgive and the perpetrator who needs to repent and be forgiven. "But God demonstrates His own love toward us, in that while we were yet sinners, Christ died for us. Much more then, having now been justified by His blood, we shall be saved from the wrath of God through Him" (Romans 5:8-9). Upon receiving Christ and being born from above, you have been washed with the blood of Jesus of all impurities (1 John 1:7) and you are now justified by God (made right with God) and are a child of His kingdom.

> *Do not love the world nor the things in the world. If anyone loves the world, the love of the Father is not in him. For all that is in the world, the lust of the flesh and the lust of the eyes and the boastful pride of life, is not from the Father, but is from the world. And the world is passing away, and also its lusts; but the one who does the will of God abides forever.*
>
> 1 John 2:15-17

CHAPTER 5

Immigrating to the United States

Growing up, there was very little to do other than going to street dances (what we might call clubs in the United States) or to church. The hope of achieving greater things and moving outside of my community seemed impossible for me. It certainly seemed like a waste of time to so much as dream of a better life.

When I was older, I tried to fit in with all the other young girls. I didn't like the way they dressed nor the way they gyrated to the new dances that were so sexually suggestive. I was very uncomfortable, but to be a part of the crowd, I believed I had to dress like them. I did whatever it took for me to fit in, even wearing revealingly short shorts and shirts. Though my parents never allowed me to attend these dances, when I became an adult, I did.

The most exciting times for me going to dances were when my sister visited from England because she was an amazing dancer. Watching her made the dances exciting for me; otherwise, I remained aloof with very little interest in this type of fun.

I enjoyed time by myself, but others saw this as a tiresome, boring way to spend time. Hidden deep down inside of me was a call that I couldn't identify. I had no idea I was included in this verse:

> And we know that God causes all things to work together for good to those who love God, to those who are called according to His purpose. For those whom He foreknew, He also predestined to become conformed to the image of His Son, that He might be the firstborn among many brethren; and whom He predestined, these He also called; and whom He called, these He also justified; and whom He justified, these He also glorified (Romans 8:28-30).

God's call can be unique; He doesn't always call the way you expect. He called me away from the lust of the world (1 John 2:15-16). I believe God protected me by causing me to be uncomfortable with the sexually suggestive dances, so I would turn away from the crowd. He works in mysterious ways, His wonders to perform.

Because of God's call, I started attending church, where I seemed to have found my home. I was free to praise God without being mocked. Therefore, I went to church every time there was a service. I believed I turned my life over to Christ in 1997, in my early twenties. Xaria was about one year old.

However, as I look back, while I felt God tugging at my heart, I had never really considered my sin and my need for repentance—prerequisites to true salvation. I now believe the local church was the draw, not so much the Lord Himself. I was baptized and immediately began working for the church. I became involved in fundraising for a much-needed new building, but where I found deep satisfaction was in leading the youth group. God was not really in the forefront of my thinking, but rather the local church's needs, and especially my beloved youth group.

When did God convert my heart of stone to a heart of flesh (Ezekiel 36:26-27)? I don't have that clear testimony of a singular event like many of my fellow followers of Christ. Rather I now believe God required me to go through the pain of the ensuing years before redeeming my life from the pit. At some point, as I cried out to Him in my anguish, He saved my soul for a life of obedience out of which serving would then flow.

Moreover, I will give you a new heart and put a new spirit within you; and I will remove the heart of stone from your flesh and give you a heart of flesh. And I will put My Spirit within you and cause you to walk in My statutes, and you will be careful to observe My ordinances.

The Lord God,
Ezekiel 36:26-27

So I became the youth president of the church, starting with approximately ten young people in a dilapidated church building. A variety of activities drew young people in from the community causing our little group to grow to one hundred in number. I was privileged to lead some very successful fundraisers, which surprisingly included many of the adults of the community.

We all participated in the building of our new church from the ground up. I saw men and women coming out in droves with wheelbarrows, buckets, shovels, and spades. They mixed cement all night, while the women cooked on a wood fire or coal stove. Work was done in a united effort to get the church completed. We are encouraged in Psalm 133:1, "Behold, how good and how pleasant it is for brothers to dwell together in unity!"

It was unbelievable—the church we lovingly built had dirt for a floor and little plywood boards nailed together for its benches. The ceiling was made of ancient zinc with big holes. Whenever it rained, it was impossible to have church, but this was our church, one we had built together, one in which we would be able to worship our Lord in community.

The church we lovingly built had dirt for a floor and little plywood boards nailed together for its benches.

†

Those young people had become more than just members of a youth department. They were like my own children. It was almost as if I had birthed them. I played an important role in their lives, which I took seriously. They believed in me and respected my position as the youth president.

It was never difficult for me to get them involved in the different church activities. For example, it was not unusual to find a strong showing of the youth for a Saturday morning walk-a-thon. We walked throughout all the surrounding communities asking for donations. At a set time, we would all meet at a predetermined location to go back home.

It was fun as we gathered all our monies from the different groups. Amazingly our community gave more than enough to hire a contractor to put a new roof on our church. In everything we did, we did it joyfully. Whatever I planned, they were all in for it. They depended on me for counseling, love, and direction.

I thoroughly enjoyed my role as youth president, but my job was another story. It did not afford me anything beyond a paycheck to paycheck existence, consequently I began considering emigrating from Jamaica to the United States where I already had family living. I wanted a better life for my daughter with Mitch, Xaria, who was about two years old at this time, and for myself. I desired the opportunities that were unavailable if I stayed in the country of my birth. I longed to work hard and be rewarded for my efforts, so I put in an application with the government of the United States.

The opportunities that lay ahead were beyond my wildest imagination, yet I had to think long and hard about such a life changing decision. What should have made me the happiest young lady in the world at the possibilities, had me crying all night.

I asked myself how I could let them down knowing I was their role model. Was it worth it to leave them? Should I go, or should I stay? There wasn't a dry eye from the day I made my decision until I left. They threw me a surprise going away party the night before I departed.

They wept so much at the party that it was extremely difficult for anyone to have fun. I wanted so much to change my plans and to stay, but everything was in place for me to go. In between crying, there was laughter and words of encouragement. I had no idea I meant so much to those young teens.

The next day the youth department chartered a taxi, and those who were unable to ride in the taxi took public transportation to the airport. Getting to the airport in those days meant taking two or three buses. To think they did it just for me made the moment even more bittersweet than I ever could have imagined.

Worried about the children, I was afraid that they were going to accept life in the community for what it had to offer, which was almost nothing. The majority of the youth group came to the airport to say good-bye. It was very hard for me.

I could not believe they went the extra mile to get to the airport to say another good-bye and to cry another tear. The heartfelt sentiment they showed towards me was priceless. My experience with these young people gave me confidence in working with other people whether young or old. I realized that my compassion and my love for people were beyond what I could control. There is nothing too good that I would not give to someone in need. I developed a passion for lost souls even though, as I look back, I am reminded that I was once a lost soul too.

And who of you by being worried can add a single hour
to his life? And why are you worried about clothing?
Observe how the lilies of the field grow; they do not toil
nor do they spin, yet I say to you that not even Solomon
in all his glory clothed himself like one of these.

Jesus, Matthew 6:27-29

CHAPTER 6

Living by His Rules

Living with Rob included living by his rules. One of them was that I could never have anyone over to our home except my siblings. I was living like a prisoner with limited visitation rights.

I remember an incident when a girlfriend from Jamaica called for my help in her hour of need. My friend's son needed serious medical attention. Monies were raised for the surgery and transport to the United States, but my friend needed a place to stay. Without hesitation, and without consulting with Rob, I said yes.

My "yes" to her left me in deep stress for days, but knowing her situation, I could not take it back. So for days I tried to gather the courage to talk to Rob about her, but like a child, I twiddled my thumbs and said nothing. Hoping that her urgent situation would spark a sense of compassion from Rob, I found the courage to tell him the day she was due to arrive from Jamaica. He was furious, to say the least. He made it very clear that my friend and her son were not welcome in our home. Our conversation took place hours before she landed. They took a cab from the airport and arrived at my house. I was extremely happy to see them, but very nervous.

When Rob came home, his heels were dug in; he was unwilling to change his mind on the matter. My friend and her sick son finally left our home hours later, the same day they had arrived. My heart was broken, and I cried all night. At that moment, I truly felt like death would have been better for me.

> *At that moment, I truly felt like death would have been better for me.*
>
> †

I was embarrassed to know this was the reality of my life and was very concerned about where my friend was going to stay. She never even slept at my house, not once, and that broke my heart into pieces. One of my family members eventually agreed to take them into their home.

I thank God for making a way for her out of a seemingly hopeless situation. After that I decided I would never have anyone visit me again, except my siblings. I was tired of learning some new aspect of Rob's character, because I was always disappointed. My life revolved around Xaria—and Rob when he was in town.

I had accepted my life the way it was. It wasn't long after the incident with my friend from Jamaica and her sick son, that I faced another dilemma. Once again, someone close to me needed housing. I received a call from a cousin, with whom I was very close. She told me her sister needed somewhere to live. I thought to myself, *is this a test?* The truth was

I needed the company; I needed a friend, someone to trust. I was tired of bottling up all my pain and frustration. I felt like it was about to burst inside of me.

One of my cousins, who eventually became my tower of strength during many events in my life, needed my help. She was down and out, and I was her last hope. I wanted to help, but how? I knew I couldn't go back to Rob again, asking permission for someone to move in with us, even if it were for just one day.

I prayed fervently about approaching Rob regarding my cousin's situation because of what had transpired with my friend. I remember approaching Rob with a thousand pleases before even asking him his permission.

I was afraid to ask, and he knew it. I begged him not to say "no!" To my surprise, when I talked to Rob about my cousin, after a few questions and a stern warning, he agreed. I think he agreed because of divine intervention, and maybe he felt guilty about my friend and her son. I thought to myself, *who is this?* It was like I was dealing with a different person. His response to me was "one to three weeks only." It didn't matter why he said "yes," all I knew was a light bulb of joy lit inside my heart.

Ultimately, she lived with us for three years. When my cousin came to live with us, it was more beneficial for me than it was for her. During her stay with us, she witnessed several fights between Rob and me. She bravely took many punches for me, both figuratively and literally.

As I sat on the sofa crying after every encounter with Rob's fist, she was there to comfort me. She would sit and listen with an attentive ear, because she knew and understood my situation. Let me encourage you that God knows exactly what you need before you ask. I thank the Lord for this dear friend.

When God says that something will be done, it's done.

Don't think for a moment that my cousin coming to live with us was Rob's compassion in any way; it was without question the will of God. If you are going through something right now, be patient because you will see the provision God has prepared for you.

> *Where can I go from Your Spirit? Or where can I flee*
> *from Your presence? If I ascend to heaven, You are there;*
> *if I make my bed in Sheol, behold, You are there. If I*
> *take the wings of the dawn, if I dwell in the remotest*
> *part of the sea, even there Your hand will lead me, and*
> *Your right hand will lay hold of me.*
>
> David, Psalm 139:7-10

CHAPTER 7

Doubts and Fears

While my professional life was successful, my personal life was in shambles. Many days I closed my office door behind me, and my smile would fade with the turn of the key. The thought about going home at the end of the day brought tears welling up in my eyes. I wanted to turn back the hands of time and erase Rob from my life.

My daughter had the security of a comfortable home that I had always wanted her to have. But what type of security? Xaria watched as I was verbally and physically abused by this man from whom I believed I was incapable of breaking away. There were times when my daughter not only observed my manipulation and mistreatment but experienced her own at the mouth and hands of this controlling man.

Security? We had no security at all. We were imprisoned in the cell of my acquiescence. True security is peace, joy, and contentment in the Lord. It took much pain and struggle for me to both realize the harm I caused my daughter and to share it with you. It is painful to admit to having brought an innocent child, whom I love desperately, into the web of my choices.

My daughter and I were imprisoned
in the cell of my acquiescence.

†

People who didn't know my story would be envious, while others would say, "Girl, you are blessed." Really? Blessings are measured by the depth of your joy, not by the accomplishment of material gain. This is just a bonus. I wanted to return everything I had acquired because it was of the devil and my own sin nature, but doubt and fear had me bound.

Like a person straitjacketed in a cultic system—be it religious or not—I could never do enough to please Rob. I allowed him to isolate me from family and friends. If we disagreed, his way was the right way; I lived in fear of his reaction to whatever I said or did. While I had financial security, which was a far cry from my life growing up in Jamaica, my burden was heavy and my yoke oppressive (Matthew 11:30). We lived together and worked together. I could find no dignified way of extricating myself from my situation, let alone find the will to do so, as I was so completely under Rob's control. This is not to absolve myself of responsibility, but to explain the depths to which I had fallen. And I was to fall deeper still …

Doubt and fear have the power to hold you hostage. I was no longer so afraid of losing my security, but rather I was afraid of Rob's rage if I tried to leave. While doubts and fears have the power to hold you hostage, if you believe the Word of God, you will realize that even when you're living the reality of the situation, you continue to be free in Christ as a child of God. As I turned my life back to God, I experienced freedom within me. "For I am confident of this very thing, that He who began a good work in you will perfect it until the day of Christ Jesus" (Philippians 1:6).

I thought Rob was my sustainer, but time proved me wrong. God is the only sustainer we have (Psalm 54:4). My mistakes followed me for many years. I felt like I was living in a maze—the deeper I ventured in, the more lost I became. So how could I get out? Turning back was not an option, so I kept moving forward but with a new attitude.

I kept moving forward but with a new attitude.

†

I moved forward with faith in Jesus, and I knew without a shadow of a doubt that He would lead me to the way of escape. In a maze, there is but one path by which you enter and only one path by which you are able to flee. But there are many twists and turns along the way which lead to dead ends, and if you're not careful, may cause you to give up. That's exactly what the enemy wants you to do. Perseverance is paramount. Keep moving; you are closer to the exit than you think. Remember that as a believer, Jesus is with you always, and He will deliver you from the hands of the enemy.

I discovered I was pregnant. I immediately had doubts about having the baby due to everything I had experienced during the rocky course of our relationship. I concluded it was best to terminate my pregnancy after Rob suggested I get an abortion. I thought to myself, *what am I going to do? Where are Xaria and I going to live?* Even with the decision to have an abortion, I was left with emotional as well as material ties to Rob that were too painful to let go. I had not yet given up on the pipe dream of him changing like an ugly duckling into a swan.

It was a very difficult decision to make, but I knew he was

not interested in our baby and wanted it taken care of immediately. I eventually gave in on my own accord and decided it would be easier to cut all ties with him. Therefore, I thought the abortion would be the right thing to do in accomplishing my goal and gaining my freedom.

I slipped in and out of trusting the Lord quite often. Every step in my life seemed to be not only a decision, but also a test. In this situation, my faith dwindled as my fear increased once more. Why? Because I focused my attention on the wrong things, and not on Jesus.

When Peter focused his attention on Jesus, he was able to walk on water, but when he started to see the contrary wind and looked away from Jesus, he started to sink. (Matthew 14:22-33) This is what Satan wants. He likes the contrary wind; it's a means to cheat you of your faith in Christ, and if you lose your faith, then what do you have? Faith in Jesus is more powerful than money and will open doors that no tangible force could ever open.

I decided to move in with a friend after the abortion and made the necessary arrangements. It wasn't the best choice, but it would be better than the hurt and loneliness I felt continuously. I knew that if I lived with a friend, it was going to be temporary, because the last thing I wanted was to create any inconvenience for anyone. There would be no turning back once I made the decision to leave Rob. I needed a temporary place to stay, a place to heal. The decision to leave Rob meant that no matter how bad things would get, I knew there would be no turning back.

I remember the night before my abortion appointment clearly, like it was yesterday. I thought about my unborn child as I looked at my stomach and I rubbed my baby for the last time. I satisfied my craving for a large, refreshing glass of eggnog—it tasted so delightful. I thought to myself, *this is the last night I'll have this craving.*

A couple of hours later I opened the refrigerator. Looking for something cold to drink, my eyes fixed on the beer staring right back at me. For a second, I had a conversation with myself. I decided that the beer was not the right choice just in case I changed my mind about the abortion.

But after thinking about it, I came up with one conclusion—the abortion is inevitable. I finally gave in and started to drink the whole bottle of beer. With every sip I took, a tear dropped from my eye as I sat alone at my small kitchen table. At that moment, reality set within the core of my soul: after my appointment tomorrow, I wouldn't be pregnant anymore. This thought made me weep loudly.

> *For You formed me in my inward parts; You wove me in my mother's womb. I will give thanks to You, for I am fearfully and wonderfully made; Wonderful are Your works, And my soul knows it very well. My frame was not hidden from You, When I was made in secret, And skillfully wrought in the depths of the earth; Your eyes have seen my unformed substance; And in Your book were all written The days that were ordained for me, When as yet there was not one of them.*

David, Psalm 139:13-16

CHAPTER 8

Near Disaster

The appointment finally came for me to end the life of our unborn child. It was one of the saddest times of my life. I was already feeling little butterflies moving in my stomach, and it felt like a plea from within screaming, "I'm alive, I have a future!" It was a very difficult decision, but I believed I had made the right one at the time.

I wanted to keep my baby, but I had too many unanswered questions. Rob drove me to the clinic without saying a word. After we got to the clinic, I waited for him to say something, but he said nothing other than, "What time should I pick you up?" If he only knew how much my heart ached and how desperate I was to keep my baby. He drove away and left me all alone as I walked into the building. I felt so isolated, like an island in a vast sea of unhappiness and pain.

I entered the building, registered, and paid the necessary fee, after which I went to the back and took a seat. I sat far away from everyone, so I could be alone. Tears constantly welled up in my eyes. I looked around at the other women and there was no one else teary-eyed. *Stop it*, I kept silently telling myself. *Please stop it!*

Frankly, I needed help. I needed a voice of reassurance. I was too weak to save my unborn child. The thought of having the abortion was horrifying to me. I was already in love with my baby. The nurse came over to me and gave me some pills.

Still waiting for that improbable call from Rob, I was hesitant to take them, so I asked the most inane question ever, "Will this hurt my baby?" She looked at me with the oddest expression on her face. Then I said, "What a stupid question, huh?" I quickly took the pills to convince her I was serious about my decision. She hastily walked away with the same peculiar look on her face.

Finally, it was my turn to go in. To ease my mind, I kept saying "It's only a clot. Tomorrow I won't think about it. Soon this will be over." Those words were my anthem which made me sicker than sick. I could not find comfort in the lie.

Tomorrow was not going to be better. This was my child and not a clot of blood. I kept my phone on just in case Rob would call and say those magic words I desperately wanted to hear, "Don't do it." At that moment, while lying on the bed with both eyes filled with tears spilling over onto my cheeks, I concluded that Rob did not want our baby.

The doctor entered the room followed by two nurses. The time had come. A part of me was forced to be ready, and the other part was yearning to give my child a chance at life. In the midst of my thoughts, a third nurse came in briefly, whispered something to the doctor, and he excused himself.

The remaining nurses also followed him out of the room and I was left alone. Seconds after their departure, my cell phone rang. Thinking it was Rob, I quickly jumped off the treatment table, but it was my cousin. I was so disappointed. She said repeatedly and passionately, "Don't do it. Think about it. I know how you feel and what you are going through. I will be there for you."

I was hesitant, but she kept repeating those words and they rang loudly in my ear. I craved to hear them so badly that at this point it didn't matter who said them. Knowing someone was willing to stand with me and fight for my unborn child gave me hope.

In a split second, I was off the phone, dressed, and out the door I went. The nurse was heading back to my room, and when she saw me leaving, tried to stop me, but I said, "I've got to go," and I took off running. I felt like I was running for my life. Indeed, I was running for the life of my child. I left the money I had paid and didn't think twice. I wept as I ran, taunted by the unanswered questions. Don't underestimate God and overestimate your problems. He said He'll never fail us nor forsake us and He means just that (Deuteronomy 31:6).

I thought I was alone, but the Holy Spirit was right there all the time amidst my situation. Just in the nick of time He allowed my cousin to call me and that call saved my baby's life. I praise Jesus often for His gracious mercy in rescuing my precious son and in rescuing me from an unholy decision.

I was in a horrible situation and it seemed like there was no one around to help, but God was working behind the scenes. I just wasn't aware that He had already worked everything out for me. His Spirit is omnipresent, everywhere at the same time. Remember, God is doing more than you can think or imagine according to the power that works within us, that is the Holy Spirit within the follower of Christ (Ephesians 3:20).

God's peace is not as the world gives (John 14:27). You must trust Him regardless of what you are able to see. After spending some time weeping on the side of the road, I finally called Rob and told him I did not go through with the abortion. He came to pick me up and we went home.

We drove home in utter silence. I couldn't believe he didn't ask why I had changed my mind. Do you see God in all of this? Not even Rob could say anything about the decision that God had made.

Like a snowball rolling down a hill,
events and decisions accumulated layer by layer,
trapping me deeper into the relationship.

†

Like a snowball rolling down a hill, events and decisions accumulated layer by layer, trapping me deeper into the relationship. I didn't leave Rob to move in with my friend—there had been no abortion, thank the Lord. I kept living, sometimes barely, but I stayed before God day and night for my baby's sake. Rob went with me to my doctor's appointments, but for the most part, it was the promise that my cousin made and kept, to always be there for me, that sustained me.

She was literally like a surrogate father to my unborn child. Her support was never ending and pulled me through some very tearful and heartbreaking moments.

For many months, I was afraid of what I might have done to my unborn child. I constantly remembered the pills I had taken at the clinic in preparation for the abortion. I didn't know what the effects, if any, were going to be. I prayed fervently for God to forgive me and to let my baby be born perfect, yet I had learned that God is not my errand boy; there were no guarantees that He would accede to my desperate cries.

What was going to be my punishment? The walls were closing in on me. I was experiencing a troubled pregnancy, but I dared not share my worries with anyone. Truthfully, I was afraid of what others might say.

I had learned that God is not my errand boy.

†

I spent months tangled up in fear that my baby may be deformed. What would I tell him or her? How would I explain to my baby, "I never wanted you, and then I changed my mind and wanted you?" Would I be honest, or would I hide the truth that I am responsible for his or her deformity? I didn't know how much damage the pills had done. As the time for delivery grew closer, I experienced a mixture of emotions, both joy and fear.

My pregnancy was an emotional roller coaster for me. There was no excitement from Rob at all. I was constantly tearful with blood running from my nostrils every time I cried. At times, the devil tried to provoke my thoughts, to make me think I should have gone through with the abortion.

A few months later, it was time for the delivery of my son. The moment of reckoning had finally arrived, and the unknown would now become reality. Lying on my back, getting ready for the caesarean, tears flowed from the corners of my eyes. I was afraid, so very afraid. At that moment, I relived everything that had happened at the abortion clinic, as well as the alcohol that I had consumed the night before the abortion appointment.

I heard my heart beating loudly through the monitor. What was I going to see and hear of my baby? After a while my beautiful baby boy was finally here. I heard his cries and my first thoughts were, is he okay? Does he have ten fingers and toes? Are there any birth defects?

All these questions came pouring out of my mind. I needed to see him. "Nurse, can I please see my baby?" His Dad was there, and I asked him to hold the baby close to me, so I could look at him. My baby was perfect. I touched his little fingers and toes as I counted them and felt his face against mine.

I sobbed with thanksgiving to God for what He had done for me and my beautiful baby boy. If I had not taken the pills and my child had been still been born with a birth defect, I would have loved him regardless. But I could not have lived with myself if he had been born that way because of something I had done. Sin is like a grenade, ejecting shrapnel outward to all who are nearby.

It's amazing how God showed up and saved my baby's life with just one phone call. What if the doctor had not stepped out of the room? What if the call from my cousin had not come in? What if the doctor had remained in the room, the procedure would have started, and I would not have been able to take the call? Isn't God awesome? He is the only true conductor of our life.

God has a plan for every child.
†

God knew my baby before he was formed in my womb and He knows the plans He has for him (Jeremiah 1:5). "'For I know the plans that I have for you,' declares the Lord, 'plans for welfare and not for calamity to give you a future and a hope'" (Jeremiah 29:11).

No matter what your circumstances, choose life for your baby and choose life for yourself. God has a plan for every child. Whatever you are going through, choose life. I hope one day my son will understand and forgive me. I hope he will never think, even for one minute, that I loved him any less. Sometimes it hurts to think of what I almost did to him. Whenever I feel this way, I always give him a tight hug and remind him of how much he means to me.

If you are going through the same situation, where the father doesn't want your child and you feel like you have no other choice, please choose life.[1] The decision to choose life is yours, not his. You have no idea who God may birth through you. And do consider adoption as another viable alternative.

Just imagine, one phone call saved my baby's life, just one. This was not an ordinary call. This was a supernatural, divine intervention by God. I encourage you—don't hesitate to call someone if God puts it in your spirit. You may just save a precious life, one created in the image of God.

1   Care Net, 44180 Riverside Parkway, Suite 200, Lansdowne, Virginia 20176. Phone: 703.554.8734. Email: infor@care-net.org. Website: https://www.care-net.org/find-a-pregnancy-center.

For what does it profit a man to gain the whole world, and forfeit his soul?

Jesus, Mark 8:36

CHAPTER 9

A New Beginning, Yet No Changes

The birth of our son brought unspeakable joy to our relationship. It's amazing that what Rob thought should not have been became the center of his world and mine, did indeed take center stage. Our relationship during that time was exactly what I wanted, except we weren't married.

Life had taken a fresh twist with our new bundle of joy arriving on the scene. We did have one thing in common—the unconditional love we had for our new baby boy. Rob also started a father-daughter relationship with Xaria which for her was a struggle to accept since all she had experienced until this point was Rob's wrath. I had a glimmer of hope that life was going to get better for us.

Rob was always a good provider for his children. After Dante's birth, I bonded with Rob in a totally different way. Our son was the adhesive that held the relationship together. Regardless of what we went through, with the birth of our son, our liaison took on a new meaning for me.

I watched him play, feed, and bathe Dante on a regular basis. Many nights Rob would let him sleep on his chest. What a beautiful sight! Seeing how he cared for our son gave me hope that we could become a true family; I thought that Rob would finally want to settle down.

However, I soon learned that the other woman was not out of the picture. The private conversations between Rob and her continued, making me feel disrespected in my own home. As painful as it was, I had accepted them. Little did I know—and am <u>still</u> not clear about—that there were other women and children in our tangled web of deceit.

While Rob had become a loving father to our son and "step-father" to Xaria, his other troubled behaviors remained the same. I realized that if I didn't get out, I would wind up in an unhappy, abusive relationship for the rest of my life, and my children would be subjected to this unhealthy situation in which I had put us. My tears and arguing were not going to change him. Often I asked myself, *how did I get into this mess?*

I was happier sleeping on my blue towel and cleaning the toilets in that restaurant long ago before I met Rob. Having nothing with God is better than achieving the whole world without Him. "For what does it profit a man to gain the whole world, and forfeit his soul" (Mark 8:36)? I desperately needed God's direction. I was living with one foot in the Lord's kingdom and the other in the world.

I was living with one foot in the Lord's kingdom and the other in the world.

†

Loneliness and a broken heart almost drove me into another relationship. Sin can surely take you further than you expect to go. I had looked to another man for comfort. I was lost, confused, and desperately wanted to leave Rob, but I did not have the strength to do so.

I started talking on the phone with another man who made me feel much better about myself. Even if every flattering statement he told me was a lie, I didn't care. I wanted to hear the lies anyway. Let's face it, I needed to hear his complimentary words. I felt totally neglected by Rob.

I was not in an intimate relationship with that person. To be honest, it probably would have led to that if Rob had not found out beforehand. What a mess! Now I was going to attempt to use one sin to deliver me from another. Can sin deliver you from sin? No! Only God can. Many people who refuse to wait on God have lost their very lives because of lack of patience and therefore acting outside of God's protection.

Not every mistake has a quick fix. Life is so much better when you wait on God. It doesn't matter how things look, just wait on Him. A lot of the pain and heartache I experienced was not because God was not working it out; it was because I had my own agenda.

A lot of the pain and heartache I experienced
was not because God was not working it out;
it was because I had my own agenda.

†

Often, I tried to fix the situation with no success. After witnessing me having a conversation with my male friend, Rob thought there was too much laughter between us. He concluded that he needed to start spying on me.

Once he found out about the other man, things got a little crazy between him and me. He started recording every phone conversation, requesting the call detail statements from the phone company, and watching every move I made. He had become a private investigator. He was so vindictive that he took the recordings and played them for people I knew in the business community to embarrass me. Finding out about this other person was very devastating to him. Why? Was I his trophy?

Is this the unfairness of life? Somewhere out there he had other women and children. He had some nerve to be jealous. We went down a rocky path of deception and cruelty which was not a pretty sight. Rob was constantly breathing vicious and nasty threats which scared me. I thought he would kill me like in all those Lifetime movies I had watched.

I had no choice but to wait on God to make a way of escape for me while I accepted life as it was with Rob. Every two weeks he had to go out of town, no matter what. When he went on his little excursions, I was left home alone with the children.

I kept all the pain to myself and never shared it with my family or friends, except for my cousin who lived with me. I did not want them involved until I found the strength to walk away, which I never did. There is a set time for your deliverance and it will be great. Trust God!

> *For that man ought not to expect that he will receive anything from the Lord, being a double-minded man, unstable in all his ways.*
>
> James 1:7-8

CHAPTER 10

Growing Wings

After a few years, when my cousin moved out, my Mom came to live with us. My Lord Jesus knew I needed someone to be there with me and to be my strength when I was weak. I told her the same story I told everyone else when Rob went away. As close as I am to my Mom, I never got her involved. She loved and trusted Rob like her own sons.

Both she and my Dad thought he was such a good man, and I kept it that way. I never shared any of the physical and verbal abuse with them. They thought I was happy and I really was, but it didn't come from the source they had imagined.

My Mom was not seeing happiness as she perceived it; rather she was seeing the peace of God in me. The curious thing was I started to cope very well when Rob went away on one of his excursions; I didn't miss him as much as I used to. I was deeply concerned about my life with him. Yes, my faith was strong in the Lord, but I still had concerns about living in sin.

I wondered when he would realize that he needed to settle down, or set me free, if I wasn't what he wanted. With my Mom living with us, I started growing wings to fly.

Rob wasn't taking care of the home like he had his family living there. Everything was basic. I watched all the other investment properties get refurbished and they looked so much better than where we lived.

I became very frustrated one day and told him I was going to purchase another home in which we would live. Of course he did not believe me and thought I was joking. There is something about growing wings—they usually do not show on the outside, but you feel them growing on the inside. Rob had a surprise coming his way.

There is something about growing wings:
they usually do not show on the outside,
but you feel them growing on the inside.

†

I went out searching for another house to call home, yet he never came with me. He really did not think I was going to do this without him. He was so used to having this predictable woman around him, one who always needed his approval. To his surprise, I placed a contract on a home that I really loved. I was maturing and becoming my own person. Prayer changes things.

I can't believe I did it without him. Every step of the way, I prayed. I was nervous as a cat and afraid even to sign the contract, but something kept me going. It was God who kept me going. It was really happening, a contract on a home that I loved. Wow!

By the time Rob knew I was serious, it was too late to stop me. Knowing his ego, he was not going to join me and the children in our new home. He had to be "the man—the macho man." I was going full steam ahead, even though I was nervous embarking on the home buying process alone. The wings inside kept me growing; you fly even when you are afraid.

I used the money from an investment property for my down payment. While going through the inspections and everything that pertains to purchasing a home, my heart ached that Rob still did not flinch. He was standing on the sidelines waiting for me to fail. The Holy Spirit empowered me, and I walked through it with God on my side to the very end. Every step of the way I prayed about everything. The flesh side of me questioned how I could do this without Rob. I eventually closed on the house, received the keys, and moved in. I hoped it would become our home.

I moved everything from the previous home, including Rob's things. He came and picked up everything that belonged to him. At that moment, I gave him every opportunity to make it right. All I wanted was to keep my family together, but Rob's heart was hardened.

Was this my opportunity to live without him? Maybe, but I did not take it. How foolish can one be? Your flesh will cause you to act foolishly. Can you say, "blinded by love?"

Eventually he started coming around, and after about four months, he finally moved in little by little. He was very uncomfortable and unsettled. He never once called the home, "our home."

He would always say "your home." This indicated we were not unified in any way. I continued to keep silent because I knew the home was God's gift to me. I believe God was creating the separation between Rob and me that I both longed for and feared during that time, but I couldn't—or wouldn't create it for myself.

I trusted my eyes which could only see as far as the present. What a failure in doing so! Wavering faith is very dangerous, and I found myself in and out of it continuously. I did not trust God, perhaps because I could not see what He was doing at the time. The thought of being a single mom scared me. It is a failure of faith to believe God today and doubt Him tomorrow. Hebrews 11:1 states, "Now faith is the assurance of things hoped for, the conviction of things not seen." The responsibilities I would soon face are those I was supposed to have faced at this point. It's important to be firm and steadfast in being obedient to God's will.

One day I wanted Rob out of my life, and the next day I was scared to death to leave him. This is what wavering faith does to you. James 1:7-8 tells us, "For that man [the one who doubts] ought not to expect that he will receive anything from the Lord, being a double-minded man, unstable in all his ways." God brought about the change for which I was looking, but it was going to be a different change than for what I had asked.

My unstable mind would never let me be free. After closing on the house, I should never have looked back. I was like Lot's wife, looking back with lust for the things of this world (Genesis 19). God gave me a home and what did I do? I worried about the mortgage and how I was going to sustain my family as a single mom. Instead of worrying about the bills and the children, I should have trusted God completely from the start. God will give you a choice before He acts in your situation. What I had feared initially, I still had to face. What enlightenment! God had had the answer from the beginning.

Before you get into a tug a war with God, let go and let God. In the end, He will prevail. Because of our free will, we can say "no" to God. The difference between now and then is that I am free, and I don't feel any guilt living outside of Rob's world. The battle becomes more challenging when you interfere with God's plans.

> *Now to Him who is able to do far more abundantly beyond all that we ask or think, according to the power that works within us, to Him be the glory in the church and in Christ Jesus to all generations forever and ever. Amen.*
>
> Ephesians 3:20-21

CHAPTER 11

Pain as My Training Ground

You have more strength to face your fears than you know. Walk into your God-designed destiny and don't look back. Shortly after Rob moved into the home I had purchased, I became pregnant. I was extremely devastated to know I was pregnant with twins.

Oh no! Not another unplanned pregnancy. Planned or not I had no thoughts of having an abortion.

With my first pregnancy, my ex-boyfriend Mitch was extremely happy about my pregnancy and our daughter. With my last three children that Rob and I had together, we barely shared any experiences at all. I went through the pregnancy with the help of my Mom and I hid so much heartache. I was a lonely mother, very unhappy and worried all the time. Life was a vicious cycle for me, a never-ending treadmill; a continuous repetition of the same mistakes.

I stayed up late nights worrying about my life and the lives of my babies. In the mornings, it was hard for me to get up, not just physically, but mentally also. My Mom played two gospel songs every morning which became my spiritual medicine. Immediately I would be refreshed, rejuvenated, and ready for battle with a smile on my face. Nehemiah says in Nehemiah 8:10, "'Go your way, eat the fat, drink the sweet, and send portions to those for whom nothing is prepared; for this day is holy to our Lord. Do not sorrow, for the joy of the Lord is your strength'" (NKJV).

Rob loved being in control of everything. For example, for weeks my family and I planned a baby shower, and at the last minute, he decided that I should cancel the shower. When I declined to cancel it, he refused to attend. I believe this was a test of my obedience to him, and when I failed, his hostility toward me increased.

I couldn't believe he would do something so reprehensible, but he did. The night before the christening, he wanted me to postpone it, yet I refused. When the pastor asked for the parents and godparents to come forward, he refused and remained seated at the back of the church. Why? I stood at the altar holding one baby and my Mom held the other. I wept as I stood there. I thought to myself, *how much more pain am I going to endure before God intervenes?*

God had interceded when I bought the house all by myself, but instead I constantly dragged Rob along and now consequences seemed to follow me with every step I made. Don't get me wrong, I love my babies, all of them, but had I left Rob after I bought the house, I would not have had to deal with a lot of situations in which I found myself.

Life was a vicious cycle for me, a never-ending treadmill, a continuous repetition of the same mistakes.

†

Please, never feel like God is not there with you or that He doesn't intervene in your situation. Think back to the times you disobeyed. I tried to fix a relationship that God had already pulled apart. I could not have carried on without God for He gave me strength. He gave me life amidst the thought that death might be a solution to my despair. God gave me my Mother as a strong tower and my pastor who vowed to stand by me no matter what. During my relationship with Rob, I never took blood pressure or anti-depressant medication, because God sustained me.

I also had my family who were a phone call away, but I kept them out of my relationship with Rob. God will always handpick the right people to help you through your situation.

I never argued with Rob. I had no time or energy. I was trusting in a faithful God, not Rob. Rob and I love our children, planned or not. Don't ask me to explain how a man who didn't want children ends up loving them completely, but he does.

He was always there loving and supportive of anything that pertained to his children. I welcomed and appreciated his attentiveness when it came to them. I could never take that away from him. He was a strong disciplinarian, but a loving Dad. Rob cuddled them tightly and after a while, he would throw them high in the air or just wrestle with them on the bed.

Whatever made the children happy was Rob's greatest joy. There was rarely a doctor's visit, school conference, or baseball game that he would miss. He was always there for every event or anything that concerned the children—except their christenings.

At dinner time, he would have one child sitting on each leg and the other eating from his plate. I was very happy to see my children so happy and spending quality time with their father. I told him many times what a great father he was, but that he made a lousy partner.

Seeing my children happy meant the world to me. I could

endure anything for the sake of my babies' joy, even if it meant that my life would remain unhappy. Rob was never there for Thanksgiving or any other holiday. He had to be with his other family while I was home with the children waiting for him. He was having his cake and enjoying it in both places.

God prepared me for the lonely times. He strengthened my shoulders to carry the burden of being a single mom way before I was alone. Some of what I was doing after his departure were the very things I had had to do on my own when he left on his regular jaunts.

In the ensuing years, I was no longer miserable when it came to Thanksgiving, Christmas, or any other important holiday. I was so used to being alone without Rob at the dinner table with my children and other family members that it no longer bothered me that he was not present. He has asked me to come and visit him on Thanksgiving Day after he left our family, but I told him "no."

I wasn't trying to be vengeful, but I don't think I should have changed my plans about having Thanksgiving dinner the way I was used to having it, just to please him. Where had he been when the children and I had wanted to spend Thanksgiving with him and I had to lie about his whereabouts? What about the many nights after Thanksgiving when I was lonely and cried myself to sleep? I reminded him that we had never spent Thanksgiving together before. I had to spend it the way I always did with the children and the rest of my family—without him.

He could make his same old phone call and wish the children and me "Happy Thanksgiving" like always. It was my family who was consistently there to celebrate with me and comfort me during those lonely times, so why leave my family to visit him?

Your pain is your training ground; be prepared for the

storm through which you are going. You may be unhappy now, trying to cope with your situation, but I promise God will navigate you through it. Rejoice in Him who is able (Ephesians 3:20).

It is in the dark places where you will grow wings to fly.

†

At times it seemed that trials and heartache were going to be my constant companions. Once I had accepted life as it was and learned to smile through it, God allowed me a 180 degree turn in my most painful situation. You may think your situation is dark and gloomy, but "Wait for the Lord; be strong and let your heart take courage; yes, wait for the Lord" (Psalm 27:14). Wrestle with Him and say like Jacob said, "'I will not let you go unless you bless me'" (Genesis 32:26). Everything you are going through is a part of your story. It is in the dark places where you will grow wings to fly.

You may not see your wings growing on the outside, but they are growing on the inside. Live through it, talk about it, write about it, and let God be glorified. Every situation or storm in your life, whether caused by God or allowed by God, is to strengthen your faith, to deepen your relationship with Jesus. Remember God is righteous and just in all His ways.

> *No one can serve two masters; for either he will hate the one and love the other, or he will be devoted to one and despise the other. You cannot serve God and wealth.*
>
> Jesus, Matthew 6:24

CHAPTER 12

My Desire to Serve God

I felt the pang of wanting more of God. The desire was great, and the call was clear. Light cannot be contained in a box—at some point it will find a way to escape and shine brightly. That's how I felt about the anointing[2] that God placed upon my life. I could not explain what was happening deep within me, but I had an increasing love for God and ultimately for His people.

As much as I loved God, my flesh loved Rob more.

†

Unfortunately, my life did not line up with the gift I was certain God had given me. I yearned for the day when I would get married and serve God in righteousness, but it seemed so out of the realm of possibility.

---

2   Strong leading of the Holy Spirit for a particular task, in addition to/ beyond the indwelling of every follower of Christ

I had a desire to fit in completely at church. I wanted the opportunity to do many things, but I could not because everyone knew I was not married to the man with whom I lived. Most of all I wanted to be holy, but sin had me bound.

I set forth my path with the decisions I had made and believed that I had to walk along that path. I felt somewhat like the prodigal son who wanted his inheritance early in life, journeyed "into a distant country," and "there he squandered his estate with loose living." He finally came to the end of himself, hungry and impoverished, he returned home, and confessed his sin to his father. The son was effusively welcomed by his father, and, with great compassion, he was celebrated. (Luke 15:11-32)

His life and mine are similar in that we had to go through difficult times toward maturity in Christ. God will always allow circumstances which prepare you for His purpose for your life. Prayerfully, you will eventually walk into the destiny He has laid out for you. If you think a situation is going well, it may not be as it seems. When you are out of the will of God, you should find your way back to Him, so you can do His will, just as the prodigal son did. Everything that looks and feels good doesn't necessarily mean that is what God wants for you.

Tithing is an important part of worship, so I remained faithful in tithing and giving of my time and talent. My giving helped to build the church and covered a lot of the expenses. Regardless of how much I gave or how faithful I thought I was to the cause of God, I felt like my soul was lost and that was a major concern for me. Being faithful to God means we should completely surrender to His will. I know now that this is an impossible task in my own strength and in fact is the ongoing process of laying down my life for my Lord. I was not at that place yet, and it took many years for me to realize I was living very much out of His will.

At times, I was offended when people who knew my situation encouraged me to accept God's call on my life. Their suggestions meant only one option—to walk away from a man whom I wanted desperately to be my husband. At what cost are you willing to listen to your flesh? As much as I loved God, my flesh loved Rob more.

I could not let go because Rob meant the world to me. I thought those people were being judgmental. On many occasions, I quoted Jesus' words in Matthew 7:1-2, "Do not judge so that you will not be judged. For in the way you judge, you will be judged; and by your standard of measure, it will be measured to you." Also, Romans 3:10, "'There is none righteous, not even one.'" I found comfort in using these Scriptures to justify my sin.

I later learned that I had taken Matthew out of context. Reading on through to Matthew 7:5, we see that Jesus was rebuking those who were judging hypocritically, that is they were condemning a person for something they themselves were doing. Later in the same chapter, Jesus tells us to "Beware of false prophets." How are we to know a false prophet except to judge him by his fruits, as mentioned in the same passage?

Jesus tells us in John 7:24, "Do not judge according to appearance, but judge with righteous judgment." Finally, Paul admonishes believers, "For what have I to do with judging outsiders? Do you not judge those who are within the church? But those who are outside, God judges. Remove the wicked man from among yourselves" (1 Corinthians 5:12-13).

God used those judgments to prick my heart. I was conflicted about whether or not I had built my house upon the rock of Christ, the truth, whose word is truth. Jesus tells a parable in Luke 6, verses 46-49, about this very issue. He begins by saying, "'Why do you call Me, "Lord, Lord," and do not do what I say?'" He goes on to compare a house built on the sure foundation of rock as opposed to one built on no foundation. Referring to the house built on no foundation, He says, "'the torrent burst against it and immediately it collapsed, and the ruin of that house was great.'" I thought I had built my house upon the rock, but had I truly?

1 Corinthians 3 expands on this concept, revealing for the believer that "If any man's work is burned up, he will suffer loss; but he himself will be saved, yet so as through fire" (v. 15). This will be the testing of the quality of a person's work for Christ. I look back now and can ask: could this have been me?

Often at our revivals, the pastor preached the clear gospel message of salvation only through Christ. This particular time, my heart was pricked. I thought, *so what will happen to my soul?* I was convicted by the gospel message. I was so backslidden and out of the will of God, that I felt like I was lost, questioning my very salvation and the value of my baptism as an outward sign of conversion. When engaged in ministry, I seemed righteous to many. However, those who knew Rob and me were aware that I was living in obvious sin. Inside, I was dying little by little caught up in this duplicitous life.

I leaned on my own understanding and found my own solution to be able to live in sin and work for God at the same time. I hatched the plan to move to another church where no one knew Rob and me. I totally ignored Proverbs 3:5, which tells us to "Trust in the Lord with all your heart and do not lean on your own understanding." We started attending another church where we could make what seemed like a fresh start. I wanted to be actively serving my Lord without making the necessary changes in my life. I bought a wedding band and introduced Rob as my husband. I convinced myself that if no one knew the truth, the truth would remain hidden.

This pleased Rob very much as he had no intention of marrying me. I played the part of a happily married woman. How many women have wanted to cover up their sin? I thought my plan of hiding my sin was going to be easy, but after a while I found out sin cannot be concealed, certainly not from God. (Genesis 3:8ff)

I was in for a big surprise. While no one knew about my sin, my conscience was a constant reminder. I didn't feel free to minister to the people of God, knowing I was living a lie. As a matter of fact, I felt worse. I deceived people who believed in me. The Holy Spirit convicted me daily for my actions. Being active in church only made me more aware of my deceit.

While no one knew about my sin,
my conscience was a constant reminder.

†

How many leaders like me, as president of the women's group, are permitted to speak from the pulpit today with their lives full of sin? How do you continue that path? Your appetite for the flesh will keep you in bondage. Looking back, I see God's mercy more than ever.

When I think about Ananias and Sapphira in Acts 5, I praise God that He extended His mercy to me. I had grown tired of living with a man to whom I was not married. I thought it would be easy to hide my sin, but it was an onerous burden. One day, the Lord prompted me to write a poem, "Brokenness," out of frustration with my life as I was living it. It was a cathartic act of creativity.

Prompted by a friend to consider song writing, I soon wrote the lyrics of a song entitled, "Don't Let Me Run Ahead of You." But of course, I was already running ahead of God.

I was like Jacob in Genesis 27 who deceived his father by wearing a hairy goatskin, whereas I wore a ring to deceive the people of God. The one thing I needed to do was also the most difficult: let go of Rob.

My flesh wanted Rob; my spirit wanted God. I wanted them both, so my life was in turmoil. At the time, I couldn't see what God wanted me to see because of the blinders I was wearing. Deuteronomy 30:19-20 says, "I call heaven and earth to witness against you today, that I have set before you life and death, the blessing and the curse. So choose life in order that you may live, you and your descendants, by loving the Lord your God," What will your choice be?

I wanted to undo my web of deception,
but pride had me trapped.

†

I wanted to undo my web of deception, go back to the church from which I ran away, and back to my pastor, but pride had me trapped. I thought running away would be easy. I realized undoing my lie would expose the truth by removing the mask I wore daily. I thought about what people would say and think about me. When I pondered everything, I came up with one foolish answer: keep living the lie. The basis of my lie was to serve two masters, which is impossible (Matthew 6:24). All this time I continued to serve in the position of president of the Ladies' Ministry, which grew under my leadership.

Don't Let Me Run Ahead of You

Don't let me run ahead of You
Just let me stay, stay at Your feet
I long to hear You speak
One word is all I need
Don't let me run ahead of You

Don't let me run ahead of You
Just slow me down, help me ease my pace
In spite of all my haste
I depend on You
Teach me day by day
To trust You more and more

Even when I go astray
You were there to show the way
You take my wrongs and make them right
And I've fallen to my knees
And I know you hear my pleas
God, just slow me down
Keep me on the ground

Don't let me run ahead of You
Just let me pray, pray at Your feet
I long to hear You speak
One word is all I need
Don't let me run ahead of you
Don't let me run ahead of you

Please, please don't let me run
Don't let me run ahead of You
I long to hear You speak
One word is all I need
Don't let me run ahead of You
Don't let me run ahead of You
Don't let me run ahead of You

But the Spirit explicitly says that in later times some will fall away from the faith, paying attention to deceitful spirits and doctrines of demons, by means of the hypocrisy of liars seared in their own conscience as with a branding iron, ...

1 Timothy 4:1-2

CHAPTER 13

Wavering

Being frustrated and tired of living a lie, I wanted to stop worshipping God, but I could not because of my profound love for Him. I asked myself several times why I was wasting time. *I'll never be free to serve Him like I want, with my whole heart.* I wanted people to be saved. My heart's desire was to introduce God to all people.

During my wavering, I wanted nothing to do with my life of fornication. The conflict between my flesh and my spirit, which felt like a tug of war within me, continued. I felt trapped in a home in which I was often miserable. I believed I should wait on God to move as I prayed. Now I look back and see God can do anything but fail. I know God's timing is perfect.

Should I have been more proactive? Perhaps. My life was a tangle of shared children, entwined jobs, and lots of powerful emotions that perhaps I gave into more than I should have. No matter through what you are going, you are not alone. Never stop seeking God because He has all the answers to your circumstances. We must remember some decisions are difficult to make. There is always a conflict between your desires and God's. If your desire is to serve Him, He will help you to do so. I'm thankful God saw my heart and did not spew me out like Ananias and Sapphira when they sinned against the Holy Spirit (Acts 5:1-11).

There are people today who sin, live with a double standard, and their lifestyle doesn't trouble them. 1 Timothy 4:2 tells us that their consciences have been seared as with a hot iron. When I arrived home from an inspirational church service, especially one in which I was active, the stark reality of my sin awaited me. I usually slumped my body onto the couch and replayed my whole life.

It was a constant reminder, *what have I done?* My deceptive plan of appearing married was not as easy as I thought it would be. Everything I did in church was a success, for example, every fundraiser was planned, executed, and supported by all the members. Quickly, the membership grew.

I believed I was powerfully led by my Lord in certain aspects of my life. I was a motivator for the oppressed and a strengthener for the weak. I asked myself several times, *how can this be? How can I serve two masters at the same time?* Often, I wept at the altar. I wanted to let go. Living that lie was tearing me apart. I thought serving God was my only desire, but I didn't know how to walk away from my sinful life. How badly do you want what God has for you? Are you willing to make the sacrifice that's needed to receive the promises of God? I've had hands laid on me and fasted several times, but my life remained the same. It was a mess. I was trying to serve two masters. If only, in deep sorrow, I had prayed David's prayer of repentance in Psalm 51, perhaps the Lord would have saved me and my family sooner from so much pain and consequence.

As I reflect on my life, I feel confident that the Holy Spirit living in me gave me the desire to work for God. The disconnect was in my lifestyle choices, and this is what other believers saw in me. I often felt rejected and unworthy.

During that time, when I was discouraged, God showed up and commissioned me to go to Jamaica. But how is it that God showed up in my most contrite and broken moment and commanded that I go to Jamaica, where no one knew anything about me, and the people would accept my preaching with open arms, without judgment?

'For My thoughts are not your thoughts, nor are your ways My ways,' declares the Lord. 'For as the heavens are higher than the earth, so are My ways higher than your ways, and My thoughts than your thoughts.'

Isaiah 55:8

Please don't hesitate when God clearly impresses on you to do something in particular because there are consequences if you choose not to obey. God chose to give me a taste of the anointing He had on my life. I obeyed God and went to Jamaica as He instructed. I have yet to see another mighty move of God like that on my life. I think He showed me a snippet of my future, but He had to better conform me to His will to fully use the gifts He had given me. He chose to show His mighty power to the world through me on this trip to the place of my birth.

People came in droves just to have me lay hands on them. After I returned from Jamaica, life could not remain the same anymore. I believe God had clearly and mightily used me for several days while ministering to others in my homeland. I knew I could not continue to live in my sinful, confused, and wholly unstable family relationship anymore. Even now, I cannot understand completely what God was doing, but that experience confirmed Isaiah 55:8 for me.

Rob and I continued to attend church together. He was committed to attending church and was always among the first to step up and help when needed. Yet everything I said became a judgment to him. My sense was that his heart of stone had not been converted to a heart of flesh (Ezekiel 36:26-27), but only God can know his heart. He seemed to have the outward trappings of a believer but not the inward conversion of the heart. But then again, who was I to make this judgment? Not only am I not God, I was leading a fraudulent life. 2 Corinthians 6:14 echoed in my head: "Do not be bound together with unbelievers; for what partnership have righteousness and lawlessness, or what fellowship has light with darkness?" For all my poor choices, I knew that I was a child of the King.

We were clearly unequally yoked (2 Corinthians 6:14 NKJV). I wanted more of God, while Rob was okay with the status quo. What do you do when you are trying to live for God, and the more you reach for Him the more your situation seems to hold you back? The entire time that I portrayed myself as being the perfect wife, I was very sad because my reality was far from the truth. I had tried to leave him a few times, but our relationship just fell right back into place. Life for me continued to be dark and miserable; everything seemed hopeless. I tried leaving him by living in another room in the same house. What was I thinking? He still controlled my life with the business we ran together, the home and children we shared. I decided to stop going to church.

What sense did it make? I was tired of fooling people and myself. A few days passed, and I didn't attend church. I gave God an ultimatum to deliver me or I was going back to my life of sin full time. What a silly thought—I was already living in sin full time. While in this flesh we all struggle with sin. However, I was being willfully disobedient and could not bring myself to make the changes necessary. When you share children with a man to whom you are not married, the waters get all the muddier. I wanted my children to have their father because in many respects, he was a good father. And, of course, despite Rob's philandering, I loved him and could not break away for my own selfish reasons.

As I now contemplate my past, where did I get the nerve to try to tell God what to do? Had I really learned that God is not my errand boy? You should be all the way in or completely out when it comes to Him. As the Lord said to the church of Laodicea in Revelation 3:16, "'So because you are lukewarm, and neither cold nor hot, I will spit you out of My mouth.'"

> ### As I now contemplate my past, where did I get the nerve to tell God what to do?

†

The more you know God, the more your conscience comes alive. Often in my past, I wished I did not know God. I wanted to erase my knowledge of Him. If I didn't know Him, I wouldn't care about the life I was living. But when He has His seal on you, to where can you run?

People talked about me, people with whom I was close, and other believers. I knew I was living with a man to whom I wasn't married. I was looked at with such disdain. I needed guidance, rather than condemnation. I wondered if they knew how much hurt I was facing, along with the excruciating pain that was engrafted in my spirit. Remember, when you see someone laughing, it doesn't always mean that they are happy. They may be suffering more then you know. These people had no idea how much I wanted to do the right thing—I simply did not see a way of escape.

I was lost and felt like a wandering Israelite going around

in circles in the wilderness of my life (Numbers 32:13). I was trying to devise a plan of escape, but I kept retracing my footsteps. I didn't seem to ever learn a valuable lesson from my actions, but rather made the same errors repeatedly.

In my heart, I knew what I wanted, but leaving or walking away did not seem like the best option for me at the time. I was right at my promised land and yet refused to take the steps required to extricate myself from the complicated situation in which I found myself. I was living with a man who emotionally and physically abused me and to whom I was not married, and yet shared children we both loved.

I chose to remain silent about God, because my life was so imperfect. I had blemishes all over me. Jeremiah, in his disappointment, said in Jeremiah 20:9, "'But if I say, "I will not remember Him Or speak anymore in His name," then in my heart it becomes like a burning fire shut up in my bones; and I am weary of holding it in, and I cannot endure it.'"

I often cried asking God to please let me go. I wanted to forget about Him, but instead every day I wanted more of Him.

Regardless of the sin in my life, I witnessed the mighty power of Jesus, fulfilling my desire to serve others and to share Christ with them. But, truly, I was concerned about my own soul. I know that God can use those of us who are not walking perfectly with Him. Are any of us? I prayed, *it's me, Lord, standing in this sinful situation, and I need to be delivered from it. I don't know how to extricate myself from this tangled web. Please help me!*

Your situation may not be like what I have experienced, but it will not change this fact: sin is sin. From my failures, I'm encouraged to share my story. Before you write your story, you must first live and experience its intricacies. When you reach the light at the end of the tunnel, you'll see that you have grown wings and you're stronger than you have ever been.

The Psalmist said, in Psalm 42:1, "As the deer pants for the water brooks, so my soul pants for You, O God." Upon reflection, I must say the Lord allowed me to live through what I did, so that today He can use me to His glory. I can now share it with the world. So, hello world!

> *The sacrifices of God are a broken spirit; a broken and a contrite heart, O God, You will not despise.*
>
> Psalm 51:17

CHAPTER 14

Walk a Few Steps in My Shoes

I may face criticism from some people, and that's all right, but one thing I have learned is that people will try to destroy you during your struggles. Not everyone will understand your failures. Sometimes it is hard to stay focused when you are failing, and people are talking about you, especially when those people are family members, friends, and even other believers. For those of you who are struggling, I pray that you will wake up and take a stand with God.

My heartache came from believers whom I encountered during my relationship with Rob. They thought they loved God more than I. They could not see I was hurting because I loved the Lord yet was so obviously not living submitted to Him. I pulled my strength from my children daily. I wanted them to be happy at all costs. I sacrificed my happiness in exchange for the happiness of my children. Being around their father was their life's joy, and I loved seeing my children joyous.

If you have experienced a path similar to mine, I pray

that, through my story, you will be empowered to make the necessary changes to bring your actions in line with God's will. Perhaps you've made some mistakes from which you believe you cannot disentangle yourself. Don't beat yourself up; we all have made grievous errors. Let me encourage you that fresh faith, joy, and strength will come with repentance, patience, and perseverance in the Lord.

As you look back over your life, you must realize it was God who brought you through all your adversities. Do you know how it feels to constantly sob at the altar, not just sob, but to wail? My daily prayer was always to serve God completely. My nightly tears were because I knew I was not in God's will. Keep yearning for God; only He knows your heart and can deliver you.

People don't know your heart, nor do they know the plans that God has for you. God is gracious even in your sin. He knows the desires of your heart. I remembered telling someone about the love of God while I was in my messy situation. I will never forget when he told me condescendingly, "Don't talk to me about God; look at you, are you better than I am?" Immediately, a bright light was shown on my reality. I thought that I had received the Lord as my Savior when I was seventeen, but still I felt so unrighteous. His words cut me like a knife. For a long time, I suffered from those words, often crying as they replayed in my mind.

It took me some time to understand that I needed true repentance through the cry of my heart for God's forgiveness. I needed to allow Jesus to be the Lord of my life. However imperfectly I was living, I was at some point justified by Christ's payment in full for my sin—past, present and future. However, He calls me to holy living which is developed in the process of sanctification, yet not fully realized until one is with Christ in eternity. The Scriptures that now give me the most security, comfort, and peace are found in the book of

Romans. Many believers call this the Roman Road because it lays out God's promises of salvation and assurance to all who believe in Christ Jesus.

Romans 3:23 tells us that everyone has sinned and fallen away from God. This sin leads to spiritual death, "but the free gift of God is eternal life in Christ Jesus our Lord" (6:23). "But God demonstrates His own love toward us, in that ... Christ died for us" (5:8). If "you confess with your mouth Jesus as Lord, and believe in your heart that God raised Him from the dead, you shall be saved;" (10:9) "Therefore, ... we have peace with God through our Lord Jesus Christ," (5:1) "Therefore there is now no condemnation for those who are in Christ Jesus" (8:1). Paul concludes by telling us, "I am convinced that ... [nothing] ... shall be able to separate us from the love of God, which is in Christ Jesus our Lord" (8:38-39).

This understanding both of salvation in Christ and the need to get my life in line with God's desires was more gradual than for some. James tells us that we must "prove [ourselves] doers of the word, and not merely hearers who delude [ourselves]" (James 1:22) because "faith, if it has no works, is dead, being by itself" (James 2:17). Yet, at the time, I was confused about my standing with God.

I thought to myself, *how do I suppress my love for God?* It was difficult to speak freely because I was living an ungodly lifestyle. Everything was a constant reminder of my living situation which I knew was outside of God's will. But what was this yearning I was feeling? In my most broken, conflicted, and disobedient situation, God was still with me. Your struggles unfold your purpose. Struggles, which are sometimes called "brokenness," can be noble and edifying. Without them you will not know God as deeply nor grow in your faith. Like a chick hatching from its egg, the struggle imparts strength.

No temptation has overtaken you but such as is common to man; and God is faithful, who will not allow you to be tempted beyond what you are able, but with the temptation will provide the way of escape also, so that you will be able to endure it.

1 Corinthians 10:13

When you see other people who are in their season of rest, don't ask God why me or why someone else is happy and I am sad. Remember you don't know that person's season of struggles. Soon you will see your light at the end of the tunnel and, while you are in your season of rest, someone else is reflecting upon your seemingly blessed life and thinking, *why me?*

Soon you will see your light at the end of the tunnel and,
while you are in your season of rest,
someone else is reflecting upon
your seemingly blessed life and thinking,
why me?

†

> *[L]et us not love with word or with tongue, but in deed and truth. We will know by this that we are of the truth, and will assure our heart before Him in whatever our heart condemns us; for God is greater than our heart and knows all things, ... The one who keeps His commandments abides in Him, and He in him. We know by this that He abides in us, by the Spirit whom He has given us.*

1 John 3:18-20, 24

CHAPTER 15

A Close Encounter with My Lord

My mother decided to spend Christmas in Jamaica and took the children with her. That was very exciting for me because Rob and I would have time together alone. It would be the first time since the children were born. Oh, I did miss them for sure, but I had a fantasy world of events planned for Rob and me, which made me deliriously happy.

Time alone with Rob at last. I was on cloud nine just thinking about it. As we approached the Christmas holidays, to my surprise, a few days after everyone had departed, he had the nerve to ask me to choose which holiday I wanted to spend with him. My choices were Christmas or New Year's Day. The other holiday he would spend with his other family.

I frowned as I looked at him in disbelief. "What do you mean?" I asked hysterically. *This is ludicrous*, I thought to myself. He looked up at me and said, "I must go, dear. At least I gave you the chance to choose the holiday."

I wanted to be his wife more than anything in the world, and he was gloating about the fact that I got to choose the holiday I wanted to spend with him. Why did I keep erasing the handwriting on the wall? I had read it so many times, but it was as if I were blind. What was it going to take for me to wake up and smell the coffee? It felt like my heart was being ripped out of my body. This was another confirmation that he had no plans of settling down with me. I didn't know if I was hurting because of him leaving or thinking, *how much longer would I choose to live in the bondage of our sin?*

Only a fool would not realize that there was another woman, but what other woman? The last I had heard it was just him and me. He had ended the other relationship. The fact that I had not received any more threatening calls seemed to be confirmation. *This was the last straw*, I thought to myself. *Do or die, I am leaving.* For far too long he kept going back and forth between our home and out of town.

I had questions. Where did he go? What was he doing? My life was a puzzle with countless missing pieces. I didn't argue because I was too weak and frustrated. Tears welled up in my eyes and were ready to drop. My heart was truly broken; it hurt to fall from cloud nine as reality finally set in.

My life was a puzzle with countless missing pieces.

†

I quickly walked to the bathroom to be alone, not wanting Rob to see me cry. I slumped to the cold, hard, tile floor and sobbed silently. My first thought was that I would be trapped for life in unhappiness and I'd never be the Christian I desired to be, not in my own strength. I was unable to speak; I could not stop sobbing. Whenever I am hurting, I go to my bathroom and just sit on the floor crying and praying. My bathroom is my safe haven, where I pour my heart out to God. I feel like my bathroom is God's meeting place with me. But this instance wasn't my usual prayer meeting. I offered up a 911 emergency prayer, because my hopes and dreams where shattered.

I felt that even God had forgotten me. I just wanted to be left alone to sob—silently! I was angry and frustrated because I had exhausted every option to get Rob to settle down. I immediately started praying. In that moment, I hated the fact that I wanted my life to be right in the eyes of God. If I could undo my love for God, that would have been the very moment to do it. That way my sin would not seem so damning.

I thought, *at what point would I choose to serve God on His terms?* I accepted the possibility that while I was saved and therefore a child of God, I might never be of much use to my Father, because I was not living a submitted life. 1 John 3:18-20, 24 says, "let us not love with word or with tongue, but in deed and truth. We will know by this that we are of the truth and will assure our heart before Him in whatever our heart condemns us; for God is greater than our heart and knows all things....The one who keeps His commandments abides in Him, and He in him. We know by this that He abides in us, by the Spirit whom he has given us."

> *It was as if I were in a burning building,*
> *yet too blinded by the smoke to see the exit*
> *and make my way to safety.*
>
> †

That night I cried and begged God to remove Rob from my life or to change him. I could no longer tolerate being out of the will of God, but I couldn't manage to locate an escape route. It was as if I were in a burning building, yet too blinded by the smoke to see the exit and make my way to safety.

While I was crying and praying, I experienced something

I never had before, at least not in that fashion. I heard a voice and it was like no other. God spoke to me <u>audibly</u>. Yes, audibly. I was so afraid yet amazed at the same time. I stopped crying and with my eyes wide open, I looked out of their corners without moving a muscle. My face was saturated with tears, gluing my hair to my face. I truly had a John 10:27 moment, "'My sheep hear My voice, and I know them, and they follow Me.'" I listened attentively to the clear and very precise voice.

I did not know how to react or what to say. I could not believe that God was speaking to me. Even though it was the first time I had heard the audible voice of God, I immediately knew it was Him. My heart was pounding so loudly that I could hear it. My sense of hearing was heightened, and I was intent on listening to what God had to say. With amazement, I asked a few questions and He answered. How can this be? Oh, my God!

As shocked as I was, I received God's instructions, which were: "I am sending you to Jamaica where I am going to elevate you." I thought quickly to myself … *Jamaica? I cannot go to Jamaica now.* But God kept speaking and I listened.

"I cannot elevate you here because people will not comprehend what I am about to do in your life. In Jamaica, you will be accepted with open arms and you won't be judged." In other words, based on His instructions, God was pointing out to me that people here in the United States, especially in my home church, saw my failures more than my love for Him. He would send me back home where people would embrace me. God is amazing—He sees the heart of man and the intentions of everyone (1 Chronicles 28:9). In that moment, and for that chapter in my life, God saw what others didn't, couldn't—or wouldn't see in me.

Elevation doesn't always come to the qualified or the equipped; it often comes to the outcast and the unlearned of those who desire Him. Then He spoke again, "I will also create a separation between you and Rob, because where I am taking you, I cannot take you like this." That statement was stunning, to say the least.

A separation! I immediately gasped for a big gulp of air and sighed deeply. I had almost forgotten I had not been breathing for a while. I was afraid and thought to myself, *God, is that You?* It was unbelievable; a mixture of fear and excitement flooded my mind.

In the first instruction God gave me to go to Jamaica, I knew it was Him speaking. But when He told me He was going to create a separation between Rob and me, I had to question this because I wondered if God knew what was at stake. My four children would not have their father, and I would be alone to raise them. Of course God knew. Frankly, I would have preferred to hear, "I'm going to change Rob."

I finally managed to get in my last question. I asked nervously, "Are you going to kill Rob?" Before I received an answer, guess who barged into the bathroom? Rob! I was so disappointed—distraught even—in everything God had said that I needed an explanation regarding this promised impending separation. Because of that interruption the atmosphere suddenly changed. I wanted to share what had just happened with him, but I was unable to explain it. I was not sure he would believe me anyway.

I kept silent and pondered on my experience much like the Virgin Mary did when the angel of the Lord visited her before Christ's conception (Luke 1:26-38). As I reflect back to that day, I realize it was God who kept me calm. Rob had no idea how much he had hurt me after he said that I had to make a choice regarding the holiday I wanted to spend with him.

Now I see God had a plan all along by showing up at the right time. He wanted the atmosphere to be conducive for the reception of His communication to me—when my heart was fully surrendered to Him. Otherwise I would not have experienced the audible voice of God. I believe there will be times in your life when God will speak to you or show you a snippet of a vision, of a future occurrence, and you should keep it to yourself, unless instructed otherwise.

I pondered everything the Lord told me. The more I thought about it, the more questions I had. How is God going to separate Rob and me? What will happen to the children? I didn't know if Rob was going to die, or what was He was planning.

I was terrified. I kept the entire encounter to myself and interceded for Rob's life daily. I went back to the bathroom, stood in the place where I often sat, and prayed and waited for God to make Himself known to me. I wanted to rekindle the conversation, but to no avail. Days went by and no audible communication was forthcoming. I had questions: What's going to happen to Rob? I didn't want him to die. *I love him, God.*

I came to the realization that God was finished talking to me. If He was not, Rob would not have been allowed to enter the bathroom, but all I saw was an interruption. Truly, who can stop God from speaking if He is not finished? I needed answers and I wanted them at that moment. The ending of our conversation left me praying more than ever for Rob. I wanted to haggle with God to change him instead of moving him out of my life. Even now I ask myself why I was so hardhearted, so invested in bargaining with God to change Rob rather than conforming my life to His will.

I looked around hoping to hear something, anything. But no matter what I did or said, I could not recover that moment of audible communication with God. I decided to watch and protect Rob like a hawk. A few days later, while at the office where we both worked, a sudden power of anointing came upon me. I looked at Rob sitting at his desk and immediately fear and a heavy burden were upon me.

And we know that God causes all things to work together for good to those who love God, to those who are called according to His purpose.

Romans 8:28

CHAPTER 16

The Turning Point

I felt the pang deep down inside. My fear for Rob was palatable. Something was terribly wrong—this I knew—but I had no clue what lay ahead. Maybe today is the day he will die in a car accident? Every time he said he had to go on the road, I wanted to go in his place. I wanted to run all his errands for him.

Rob had no idea about the fear and distress I was feeling for him and why I questioned every reason he was going on the road. At one point he hugged me and asked me, "Why are you so worried? I'll be right back." Rob was in trouble; I was convinced danger lurked at his doorstep.

After work, I rushed home quickly to make dinner. The house was quiet, and the sound of the children's laughter was nowhere to be heard; they were with my Mother in Jamaica. I had forgotten about the way I felt at the office. Rob was home and safe, just where I wanted him to be, or so I thought. I believed I could let my guard down and relax. My constant obsession about Rob dying in a car accident could now be put to rest for the night.

"Has He said, and will He not do it? Or has He spoken, and will He not make it good?" (Numbers 23:19) God said He was going to create a separation and that's just what He meant. His plans will not be thwarted (Job 42:2) and no one can outsmart Him. He is an all-knowing God and knew exactly when to create the impending separation. The evening was quiet and peaceful. I felt the tranquility and serenity in the atmosphere.

I took a deep breath and exhaled. It felt so refreshing. *Finally, time alone with Rob,* I thought as the cool water glided over my hands while I washed the potatoes. I savored the moment as I made plans for Rob and me. That night I wanted him to see and hear only me.

I couldn't imagine what could spoil it. Regardless of what we were going through, I was happy for the alone time. Amid feeling at peace, the Holy Spirit prompted me to tune into my favorite gospel program, but I was disobedient and didn't do it; I was in a hurry to prepare dinner. You should always be sensitive to the voice of the Holy Spirit. The disobedience of not tuning into the gospel program may have caused me to miss the very word I needed to cushion the blow I was about to receive.

As I basked in the moment, I turned around to see Rob beckoning for me to follow him. The way he was acting revealed to me something was terribly amiss. A rush of anxiety impeded my body, overpowering me totally. I dropped the potatoes into the sink with a thud and followed him to our bedroom.

Something was clearly wrong. My previous thoughts at work rushed through my mind. I could tell the situation was serious. I thought perhaps robbers were outside. I was nervous and trembling. "What is it?" I asked frantically.

Then he said, "The police are outside asking for me."

"The police! Why? What happened? What did you do?"

All these questions I asked within seconds, but there was no response from him. He just held his head down while he changed out of some old clothes he had been working in around the house. I knew they were not robbers. I was about to experience the nightmare of my life.

Then I remembered the separation that God promised. How serious was this? I didn't know, but I stared into his eyes for answers. I didn't receive a verbal response, but I could read fear and distress on his face. I felt embarrassment, disgrace, and hurt as I looked at him. I saw my life flash before my eyes. You name it, I saw it.

I ran to my bathroom and knelt on the floor crying and praying. I felt empty; my words were empty. I was confused, out of touch with reality. I continued to pray even though I had no idea exactly for what to pray. Fear etched Rob's face. At his request, I got up, dried my eyes, and hastened to the front door.

Fear etched Rob's face.

†

I was greeted by men dressed all in black, guns drawn. It was as if I were in a movie, in IMAX. There were approximately ten in total. They all had guns pointed directly at me while they shouted in authoritative voices, "Police! Get down on the floor! Get down on the floor!" Still in shock, I stood. Then someone prodded me and forced me to the floor.

I thought, this is not happening. This could not be happening to me. I wanted to call the authorities to come get the police, because they had the wrong house and family. I was helpless. In a moment, I was in handcuffs for the first time in my life. Rob entered the family room where I was lying face down, and I heard him say, "Let her go! It's not her you want. It's me."

I couldn't imagine how he felt knowing what he had to deal with. I started praying and crying, powerless to change the events swirling around me. I called on the name of Jesus loudly, fervently, helplessly. Undoubtedly God was there during that very chaotic moment in my life, but I didn't realize it. It was not an ordinary arrest.

I felt God's strong presence with me during the most turbulent moment of my life. There were many things I did not understand, one being the gift of tongues I experienced during that precise moment. The other was to declare to Rob what the Lord told me to tell him, "Do not fear man, but God." In an instant, I realized God was doing more than I could comprehend. I know He works wonders during chaos, but I wasn't sure if I should speak during Rob's arrest.

Although He had spoken audibly to me in the past, I found myself confused about the message I believed He wanted me to relate to Rob. So I kept quiet, disobeying God. That training ground of obedience and speaking the Word over a challenging situation was new to me at that time. I thought the neighbors could hear all the commotion, but at that point, it didn't matter.

As I prayed, I saw the detectives come to see who was praying. They all came in and looked over at me. It was not a show. It was real. I wanted Jesus. I wanted help and I knew the only one who could help me was Jesus. I felt like a noisy gong and a clanging symbol as in 1 Corinthians 13:1. It was like my prayers were not significant.

How was I going to make it without Rob? How was I going to make it as a single mother? The very question that had taunted me for many years now stared me in the face. Ready or not, it was not a query anymore; it was my reality.

The very question that had taunted me for many years
now stared me in the face.

†

The police concerned themselves about my welfare by attempting to calm me down. As they were preparing to take Rob away, they asked if I'd be alright left alone. I don't remember my response, I was so distraught.

I watched as they took Rob, handcuffed, out of the house. I wanted to protect him, to hold him, but I just stood and sobbed uncontrollably. Shortly after they took him outside, I ran to hug him, maybe for the last time. But they had already left the curb. Was he ever going to see this house again? I stood there and watched them confiscate both of our vehicles. I wondered, *will it be many years before he comes back?* Then I thought about our children, *what would I tell them?* I felt abandoned by the man I deeply loved.

For You do not delight in sacrifice, otherwise I would give it; You are not pleased with burnt offering. The sacrifices of God are a broken spirit; a broken and contrite heart, O God, You will not despise.

Psalm 51:16-17

CHAPTER 17

Shattered Dreams

My world crumbled, and my dreams shattered. My knees insistently gave way as I sobbed. I was helpless; there were no words to pray. I called my youngest brother immediately as I wailed in agony. He kept asking what was wrong, but I did not tell him—not over the phone. He called another brother who was close by, and they came as quickly as possible along with their wives.

My knees insistently gave way as I sobbed.

†

When they arrived, they found me lying in the shower fully dressed, water beating on my lifeless body. I suffered an internal heartache that pulsated relentlessly. I prayed and cried continuously. One of my sisters-in-law pulled me out of the shower. She hugged me and repeatedly asked what had happened, but I would not speak.

I was afraid to tell anyone, even my own family. It was

embarrassing, so I just kept crying, moaning and groaning. Crying was my only relief. After a while, I told them what had transpired, and they were in shock. They wouldn't leave me alone.

I spent the night at my youngest brother's home. When we arrived, I did not talk about the situation because I wanted to be by myself. All I could think about was how my life had been destroyed in an instant. I wasn't sure how to handle the situation. I never had had to deal with anything like this before. *Who do I call tomorrow? How will I find Rob?* All the things I had to do—and how to do them—made me cry even more frantically.

That night seemed painfully long as the day's events were on constant replay in my mind. I did not have a shortage of tears; they flowed all night. *When will I wake up from this horrifying nightmare?*

The next morning, I made a few calls and found out where they had taken Rob. He was in custody in another county. My sister-in-law and I drove to where he was located, and we waited all day to see him, but were unable to do so.

God is amazing and ever faithful. He had led my mother to take my four children with her to Jamaica for a visit with our family thereby sparing them from witnessing the horrifying event of Rob's arrest as well as its immediate aftermath. He freed me to go visit Rob while in custody and so much more. I believe He wanted me to be all alone with no distractions during this turbulent and horrific time.

Can you imagine how shocking and distressing it would have been if my children had been there to see what happened to their father? I don't believe I would have been able to handle my pain and theirs at the same time. I read the Word of God, cried, and prayed. I seized the moment to seek the Lord wholeheartedly. Even though I was in distress, I realized there is no better place to be for God to pour into my life. A "broken and contrite heart" is a prized treasure to God (Psalm 51:16-17).

A 'broken and contrite heart' is a prized treasure to God.

†

My brother and his wife wanted me to stay longer with them. I tried to avoid responding, but I needed to go home and be by myself. They didn't understand what I believed to be necessary. Being alone will bring tears, hurt, and even cause you to be afraid, but for me, the benefits far outweighed all the other options. I constantly felt like I wanted to cry, which was difficult to control in front of them. They thought being around them would help me forget, but the truth was that it hindered my ability to speak to God.

I stayed but one night, then mercifully went back to my own home.

Whenever you have a difficult situation, alone time with God is often the best solution. It's your moment to find out how truly great He is. God will never stop working on your behalf. He is faithful and He honors faith.

"'Call on Me in the day of trouble; I shall rescue you, and you will honor Me.'" (Psalm 50:15). What will help you transform from hopelessness and weakness to joy and strength in the Lord? "Rejoice always; pray without ceasing; in everything give thanks; for this is God's will for you in Christ Jesus" (1 Thessalonians 5:16-18). Through prayer all things are possible within the will of God. It is incredible what prayer can do.

Crying helps you know the extent of your pain. There is a thin line between strength and weakness. You cry because your spirit is fighting against the situation. When you accept the situation, and lean more on God, your tears will diminish.

Winning is surrendering, not to the situation, but to God.

100

The process of being broken must be completed. Remember you're the clay in the Potter's hand. Every impurity that is within you should be cleansed to make you more like Christ. Let your hurt drive you to your knees.

The sooner you realize Jesus is the rock at the center of your hopelessness, the sooner your life will evidence true transformation from weakness to strength, frustration to peace. God will use unusual situations to get your attention. Remember, in Genesis 3:2-3, it was not the fire that caught Moses' attention; it was that the fire did not consume the bush.

Once God garnered Moses' attention then He could instruct him of His plans. Your burning bush of trials and tribulations will not consume you either. Sometimes God allows situations to touch your life, not to consume you, but to get your attention and to purify you. Today, God may show up in your life in ways you do not understand in order to get your attention. The issues He may use might be physical, financial, mental, marital, or social in nature. When He shows up, do as Moses did. Turn from tending to your "sheep"; in other words, turn away from your busy schedule, as well as from trying to find a solution to your problems, and instead, focus on His instructions.

Ironically, we could say Moses was taking care of his family business, which was his job. Sometimes we get so busy with our jobs, school, and even other people's business that we tend to forget about what is truly important. Moses forgot about what was important to God. He forgot about God's people, the Israelites, and focused his attention on his own life. I've been at that very place where I turned my attention to my life, my own accomplishments, and what I yet wanted to achieve.

When God intervened, my whole world shifted out of position which created more hurt. It felt like I was going to be consumed by the fire of my trials. Before construction takes place, there is always demolition. That's exactly how my life felt. Your burning bush will bring you into the presence of a Holy God and you must fully surrender to His will and His way on the road to maturity.

Like Moses, I turned my attention to God and surrendered my whole life to Him. Whenever you find yourself thrust into a position of discomfort, do not fear. When a change in direction takes place, it will come with discomfort, which is part of the process. Your adversary will not be defeated by your fear, but rather by your faith in God as you submit to His will. As I continue my expedition through the twists and turns of life, it feels never ending. *Is there a smooth path?* I have asked this of myself often. I finally came to the realization that God had ordained and appointed me for a time and task for which I was not yet prepared.

I needed to be prepared so God had to heal my many transgressions with which I had been consumed. To be prepared for the task, my ear had to be inclined to the voice of God. How could God order my steps, if I could not hear or understand His instructions? There is absolutely no surrendering without spending time in the Word.

I needed answers and the only way I was going to get them was spending alone time with God and allowing Him to commune with me. There was a yearning, a crying inside to be alone.

So I headed for home.

Being home was extremely difficult for me, but I knew I had to face it. Everything was the same way I had left it. The dinner pots and pans were on the stove, the potatoes still in the sink, and the tools that Rob had been using still lay in the hallway.

I stared with tears streaming down my face as I sobbed helplessly. Life had changed completely for me. I sat down on the floor right where I had stood the night before, because I was too weak to walk. I could picture last night's events happening all over again in my mind. They were constantly on replay.

I walked around the house slowly and gazed at everything as if I were in a stranger's home. Last night Rob had been there, and now everything was falling apart. I thought, *how on earth will I deal with this?* As painful as it was to be alone, I did not have the desire to be around anyone. I wanted to be alone to sob, pray, and seek God. My only memories were of the arrest with guns drawn, and a level of fear I had never before experienced. I attempted to remember the laughter of our children, the moments of joy shared in our home, but it seemed like they were all erased and replaced with that horrific, surreal experience.

Sitting on the floor in my bathroom, I started turning the pages of the Bible seeking guidance from God. I thought about all I knew of God and all the testimonies I've heard about impossible situations in which other people had overcome adversity by God's providence and strength. I desperately wanted to see how God would change me and allow me to rise above my circumstances. I turned the pages and read whatever Scriptures caught my eye.

I came upon Isaiah 54 and it quickened my spirit with the peace that only God can give. Wow! Now I was giving God praises. I completely believed His Word. I wasn't just reading for reading's sake, something else was happening. I was being delivered and I knew it. I read Isaiah 54:4a which tremendously encouraged me. "Fear not, for you will not be put to shame; and do not feel humiliated, for you will not be disgraced"; disgrace and humiliation were two of my greatest fears. *What will the neighbors think? What will other people think?* After reading that verse, I rose from the bathroom floor, went outside, picked up my rake, and joyfully began taming the leaves in my front yard. I believe we need to be revived daily with the Word and prayer to embark on the trials that will come before us.

Disgrace and humiliation were two of my greatest fears.

†

Remember you are on a spiritual journey and faith in Jesus Christ is the substance that will take you to the purpose God has for you. Sometimes you will seem to run out of faith, even though it is a gift from God (Ephesians 2:8). Remember "faith comes from hearing, and hearing by the Word of Christ" (Romans 10:17).

There are times in life when you will run low on spiritual fuel. Our spiritual fuel is faith, and our fuel sources are: God, His Word, the indwelling Holy Spirit, and on occasion a word from a fellow believer in Christ.

When your car is low on fuel, you take it to the nearest gas station to fill it regardless how grubby and bedraggled the gas station appears. Likewise, you should not dismiss someone from the body of Christ who has a word of encouragement to share just because they do not carry a title. So, the next time you receive a word from someone, don't be quick to dismiss it, even if it comes from the mouth of an unlikely source, like a donkey. (Numbers 22)

So faith comes from hearing,
and hearing by the word of Christ.

Romans 10:17

Rob's brother retained an attorney and he went to see Rob. A week had passed, and I still had not seen Rob, but communicated with him through his attorney. I sent him a letter encouraging him to remain on his knees in prayer and I would do the same. He sent word through his attorney that he loved me. I was also asked to tell his brother to inform his out-of-state family not to come. I sensed that these "out-of-state family members" were in actuality the other women in his life, and he was telling his brother to prevent them from coming to his aid. However I didn't dwell on this because I had too much to do. I had learned from past experiences that if I wanted God to move, I had to let God do the work that I believed He was doing, and I would continue to spend time with Him. Being around anyone was going to be a distraction. I had to completely surrender to God.

Whenever you have a difficult—even shocking—situation, don't try to forget it. A time of solitude with God is often the only way you will get through it. Some people go to clubs, stay with family, or choose to do anything and everything except acknowledge the situation, turn to God, and pray. If you try to forget about the difficult situation in which you find yourself, what will cause you to bow in His presence? What will help you transform from hopelessness and weakness to joy and strength in the Lord?

A drastic change sometimes shakes your world and creates pain and separation. On the other hand, it can direct you to the right path, so you will be aware of your purpose in God and walk into God's purpose for your life. He desires you to be in a holy place to stand in His presence and completely surrender to Him.

> *And take the helmet of salvation, and the sword of the Spirit, which is the word of God. With all prayer and petition pray at all times in the Spirit, ...*
>
> Ephesians 6:17-18a

CHAPTER 18

The Word of God Is My Strength

Stay in the Word of God regardless of your situation. Even though you are delivered from whatever had you bound, it doesn't mean the enemy has given up on you. He wants you to think in the way that suits his purposes, and continually remind you of the people and things that have hurt you.

If Satan has more sway over you than God Himself, you will have a victim's mentality. You must remember that you are victorious in God and not a victim. A space can only be occupied by one object at a time. A mind occupied by fear leaves little room for faith. And the converse is also true: a mind occupied by faith and the things of God, has little room for fear.

A follower of Christ has "the mind of Christ," not in the absolute sense, but in the sense that he is now a redeemed child of God and seeks to appraise things spiritually. "For who has known the mind of the Lord, that he will instruct

Him? But we have the mind of Christ" (1 Corinthians 2:16). Accordingly, "a natural man [one without Christ] does not accept the things of the Spirit of God, for they are foolishness to him; and he cannot understand them, because they are spiritually appraised" (v. 14). Therefore, seek the mind of Christ, filling your mind with faith, not fear.

The Word penetrates and kills the dead things inside of you and empowers you in the things of God. At the same time, its truth goes forth, against anything that comes up against you. Use the "sword of the Spirit, which is the word of God" in your defense (Ephesians 6:17). Of the armor of God, we are commanded to take this "sword" up in order to resist evil and stand firm (Ephesians 6:13).

Jesus used the Word when He was tempted by Satan in the wilderness (Matthew 4:1-11). When you are in your wilderness experience, your only support is going to be the Word of God, prayer, and supplication. It must be engrafted in your spirit and heart for it to be effective. As we put on the full armor of God, our only offensive weapon is the "sword of the Spirit."

Jesus said He has given you power to trample on snakes and scorpions (Luke 10:19). These two creatures are very cunning and powerful when in their own territory. Your territory is not theirs; why should you let them have dominion in yours? You must use the power in the Holy Spirit that you were given.

Trials get challenging at times and you will experience the unexpected. When the unexpected happens, embrace it because it's more difficult to deal with when you fight against it. Just as you should not fight against a rip current that will make you weary and take you out to sea; don't fight against your trials. Here I found myself in that very situation—taking the bus to work because my vehicle was impounded. Many people had offered to pick me up or transport me to and from my destinations, but I choose to walk through my process.

My family was disappointed when they heard I was taking the bus. They wanted to help, but for me, I was going to stay right where God had me. I was not going to reach out for what I did not have. Was it easy? No, it was not. At times, I wanted to take the bus, ride to the ends of the earth, and escape my stark reality. This humbling was cathartic, even penitent. However, I chose not to fight against the temporary lack of transportation; I followed Christ all the way.

At times, I wanted to take the bus, ride to the ends of the earth, and escape my stark reality.

†

I tried not to cry, but the tears sometimes streamed down my face uncontrollably. After getting off the bus, I slowly walked home. I thanked God that my children were not there, but at the same time I wanted so much to have them with me. I needed a hug, a smile, and their innocent laughter. The house was dark, lonely, and too quiet without them.

When I arrived home in the evenings, I looked around thinking about what would be happening now if I had my normal daily routine to comfort me. But it was all gone. There was nothing to do and no one to look after. The extent of my heartache was unbearable. As if it wasn't difficult enough to deal with Rob being in jail, one hurt piled up on another.

The children frequently called from Jamaica where they were staying with my mother. I would dry my tears, muster up the happiest smile ever, and have a good conversation with them. Sometimes I wanted to rush off the phone and other times I just wanted to talk with them, to hear their precious voices and their laughter. When we ended the call, I was back to being alone with tears streaming down my face. About a week after Rob had been arrested, the Lord visited me again during prayer.

He told me very clearly, though not audibly, "Get up and everywhere the enemy has trotted, erase their prints." Not that the police were my enemy, but rather my home had been trod upon by strangers who had taken away my beloved man. My home was still in disarray from the night of the arrest. I looked at the time, and I saw that I was running late to catch the bus. So I thought to myself, *I'll do it when I arrive home after work.*

All day at work I was so anxious to get home that the minute I walked in the door, I dropped my bag to get the mop and bucket. And everywhere the strangers—the invaders— had walked, I mopped.

In fact, I cleaned the whole house. While cleaning, the depression lifted, and the mood in my home changed. I had a peace that only God can give (Philippians 4:7). I can't reiterate enough how important it is to obey God. You don't have to understand God's ways to obey Him—just do it.

> **Who would have thought that mopping**
> **would invoke the presence of God?**

†

Who would have thought that mopping would invoke the presence of God? My disposition suddenly changed from sad to happy, doubtful to faithful. "God has chosen the foolish things of the world to shame the wise" (1 Corinthians 1:27); what if I had disobeyed? After I was finished, I read Psalm 91, a psalm of protection, in every room of the house. The more I read it, the more I felt the peace of God infuse me. To my amazement, I could not believe I was suddenly smiling and filled with joy and peace, which only comes from God.

Everyone who called to check on me was asking what was going on. I told them I could not explain what I was feeling, but I knew Rob was coming home the next day. I made a

180 degree turn, and with my faith I was now ready to go to war. The next day he went to court. Sitting in the courtroom for the first time, there were families all around whose hearts were hurting because their loved ones had been arrested. I sat with tears filling my eyes.

Whenever I could, I went to the restroom and prayed up a storm. I intensely felt the anointing of the Holy Spirit. Rob was finally called, and they asked him some questions. Then I was called, and they asked me a few questions also, such as my address and so forth. Yes, the judge granted Rob bail which sounded like good news to me until I was told about having to go back to court later.

I realized the battle had just begun and I wasn't sure I was going to win. He was processed and released on bail. I was relieved to see him, but I did not give him a warm, loving hug. Instead I just stared with displeasure flashing on my face like a neon sign.

When we arrived home, I unleashed my anger like a lioness on its prey. I wanted to know about the other women (to this day, I am unclear about how many other women there were in our lives, or the number of children Rob shared with them). I wanted to know why I wasn't enough. As usual, he was evasive. He was more concerned that I had gone through his things during his brief absence than he was over my need for an explanation for his behavior.

> *[F]or if you are living according to the flesh, you must die; but if by the Spirit you are putting to death the deeds of the body, you will live. For all who are being led by the Spirit of God, these are the sons of God. For you have not received a spirit of slavery leading to fear again, but you have received a spirit of adoption as sons by which we cry out, 'Abba! Father!'*

Romans 8:13-15

CHAPTER 19

Manifestation of the Anointing

I wanted to take a break from what I had experienced, at least for a while. I lived in silent confusion. Rob was home pending trial but was in no shape to discuss the other women in our lives. I was concerned about Rob because he was constantly unhappy and hardly smiled. I now believed that I had to suppress all my unanswered questions. To this day, I do not know the entire story of his duplicitous life.

Helping Rob through his ordeal was my chief concern. Yet the reality was that I found myself caught in the middle. On one hand, he was going through a serious and difficult situation. On the other hand, the affairs he was having with other women were a tremendous burden on me. Just the thought of living without him, a single mother of four, ripped every organ in my body. I was his constant counselor and I prayed for him daily, continuously.

Rob had become so humble. Before I knew it, the time

for my next assignment arrived. I believe God told me I had to go to Jamaica. Leaving town was the farthest thing from my mind.

Even though Rob did not say it, God had given me discernment, and I believed he feared me leaving. He felt a sense of comfort knowing I was always praying and encouraging him. When God gave me His new instructions, it was, in my opinion, the wrong time for me. I gave Him some excuses. I said, "God, it's not the right time and I don't want to go." This went on for a week. I knew God was impressing on me to go to Jamaica, but I was being disobedient. As the deadline approached for me to leave, God's impression to go to Jamaica grew stronger and stronger.

I thought God would somehow accept my explanation of why I could not obey Him at that time. I was determined not to go and yet I believed God was determined for me to go. Driving to work one morning, I must say the Lord powerfully revealed Himself to me. I truly believed He warned me that I should go to Jamaica or there would be repercussions.

It was so profound, I shook with fear. It's a choice to obey God when He gives you an assignment. Immediately when I arrived at the office, I reserved my flight for the next day. This was unlike me to reserve a flight without discussing it with Rob first, but at this point I wasn't seeking his approval. He wanted to know why I had to go, but I didn't have an answer except that God wanted me to go.

In Jamaica, I experienced an awesome move of God; I was completely amazed. I had never been a part of anything like it before. My first encounter was in church on New Year's Sunday. I had the opportunity to minister the Word to a church packed with people. There was such an anointing moving on me; it seemed surreal. People came to the altar, some in tears, and others in awe whom I presumed were wondering, *is this Georgette?* What happened in Jamaica is beyond what I could ever explain. People came out in droves for the prayer meeting.

I laid hands on people and they fell to the ground crying. The next morning, people came to my parents' home asking me to come to their homes and teach them how to pray. They wanted me to teach them how to understand the Word of God. Some of these people went to church but were not being fed the Word nor were they feeding themselves.

There were things happening that I did not understand. I was certain the Lord had anointed me for ministry during this trip, and I would never again be the same. I spent four days in Jamaica, and even up to the last day before I left, people came for prayer. It is an understatement to say that this was an amazing experience.

When I arrived home, a call came in from someone I didn't know. The woman on the other end of the line told me that she had called a friend in Jamaica, and this friend had given her my number. This friend had told her that she believed God was powerfully using me, and that she should keep in touch with me, so she could call on me to help her with what she was going through in her life. I'm humbled that God chose me to be used in this way, and I know that the anointing would not have come without there first having been brokenness. He is the potter and we are the clay. (Isaiah 64:8)

My Mom and my children accompanied me home. I thought this would have been a comfort to me, but I felt as though I had stepped into a spiritual war zone. As I caught up with the attorney and the latest happenings of Rob's legal case, I was as busy as ever.

Sometimes I was gripped by the fear of the unknown. I kept going back to the first conversation when God had told me He was going to create a separation. I reasoned with myself that God had already created the separation when Rob was in jail for approximately seven days, but I was wrong.

During the time Rob was home, I saw a radical change in his life. His love for his family was more profound. He was more committed, first to God, and then to his family. We read the Bible together, attended Bible class and church together. Rob was very involved in helping with the church renovations. Whatever needed to be done, he was on it. I had all but forgotten his promiscuous behavior.

Yet, the one thing with which I struggled mightily, and refused to talk about with Rob, was the conception of one particular child he had had outside of our relationship which I only found out about after his arrest. I hadn't known this child's mother even existed, yet she accused me of interfering between her and Rob. As for the child, I know this child is innocent of the behavior of the adults in his or her life. Because I love God, I chose to love and be grateful for this child's life. That was the only option for me. However, I was not ready to discuss this child.

From the time I learned of this, I was in constant inner turmoil. If the judge had not granted Rob bail, which allowed him approximately two years to prove his love and faithfulness to our children and me, I would have kissed everything we had built together good-bye and moved on.

I would get up every morning,
crying before God to grant mercy.

†

I believe God allowed Rob to be released on bond to humble him and show him what his family meant to him. His case went on for a while because the courts rescheduled hearings for just about any reason, at any time. Meanwhile, I would get up every morning, crying before God to grant mercy. I remember one morning, I was praying and during my prayer for Rob not to go to prison, the Lord rebuked me.

He seemed to say, "How long must you continue with this request? How long must I wait for you to accept my plans? I will not move you forward like this." So I started praying, *let your will be done*, but in a split second, my emotions got the best of me. When I thought about God's will, it was too demanding. So I started to pray for a change of plan. I asked God, *please find an easier way*.

I wanted both Rob's plans and God's plans. If I could not have them both, I just wanted Rob. In my mind, Rob was a changed man, the man I had always wanted him to be. But having him proved not to be God's will; Rob had to go. It took some time for me to accept God's plan. In tears, I surrendered and said, *let your will be done*. That time I meant every word of it, even though it was painful.

In tears, I surrendered and said, 'let your will be done.'

†

Things finally came down to the wire. Every time there was a court date, I would be somewhat confident that it would be rescheduled.

But after God rebuked me, I felt in my spirit that the time had come, and the judge was going to make his decision soon. Just as I had thought, at Rob's next court hearing the judge ordered him to surrender in approximately one week to an out-of-state facility. It was a difficult pill to swallow. My heart was heavy in every sense of the word. Together, we were raising four children, who were between the ages of six and sixteen. They had a great relationship with their father/"step-father."

It was the weakest and most helpless moment I've ever suffered in my life. Soon I was going to be left alone, at home with four children who were depending on me to get them ready for school, to be there for them, to be both mother and father. The morning of our last full day together I literally struggled to make breakfast and be a mother. The younger children did not know what was going on.

We ate breakfast together as a family for the last time. Rob and I had tears in our eyes as the children watched. We tried to hide our tears, but it was next to impossible to do. He encouraged our children to listen to me and reminded them how much he loved them, no matter what. We played love songs and danced together.

I rested my head on his shoulder and tightly wrapped my arms around him. It was not easy; everything we did we knew was for the last time, and we wanted to do so much more. Soon he would not be there when I arrived home from work, shopping, or taking the kids to their many practices. I could call his cell phone, but he would not answer. Fear gripped the very core of my being.

In the evening, after the kids were asleep and the quietness of the night stole my thoughts, I wanted to quickly flip the pages of my life to see how the story would end.

I wanted to quickly flip the pages of my life
to see how the story would end.

†

> *And He has said to me [Paul], 'My grace is sufficient for you, for power is perfected in weakness.' Most gladly, therefore, I will rather boast about my weaknesses, so that the power of Christ may dwell in me. Therefore I am well content with weaknesses, with insults, with distresses, with persecutions, with difficulties, for Christ's sake; for when I am weak, then I am strong.*
>
> 2 Corinthians 12:9-10

CHAPTER 20

The Separation

Sometimes your life's journey is best walked alone. Abraham's journey to mount Moriah was lonely. In the early morning, he left his camp with his beloved son Isaac, as well as with two of his servants. Yes, he had three other people with him, but that had to have been a very solitary journey because he couldn't share the purpose of the trip with anyone (Genesis 22:1-14).

I believe Abraham, even though he had faith in God, was fearful of the unknown. He was prepared to sacrifice the son he loved, his promise from God, yet he trusted God to provide. Every step he made took him further from home and closer to the place of sacrifice. At the last moment, God provided a ram for His required sacrifice.

As you travel along your life's pilgrimage, you must learn to flow with the tides and dance with the waves. Trust Christ and be patient in your time of adversities. The day before

Rob had to report to the authorities to start serving his sentence was very arduous for me.

*... you must learn to flow with the tides
and dance with the waves.*

†

The evening before Rob was to report to the authorities, I needed a miracle, and I cried all night, which didn't change a thing. I wanted God to alter His plans to include Rob in the equation of my life. My heart was broken, and only God could heal it. *How am I going to make it?*

I remember Rob's final morning at home so vividly as he prepared to leave to surrender his freedom. My freedom was also taken when he left. It was the last time for him to sleep in our bed, to have breakfast in our dining room, and to take a shower in our bathroom.

I can only imagine how family members with someone in hospice or being taken off life support must feel. I felt like my world was on life support. I felt hopeless, but I knew it was God's will. I remembered once again God impressing upon me during my prayer time that He would put a separation between us and He did. "For I the Lord will speak, and whatever word I speak will be performed" (Ezekiel 12:25). I waited for a miracle.

I could not believe that as of that day I was going to be a single mother. A part of me died while the other part struggled to stay alive and be strong for my four beautiful children. How was I going to get through this? I looked at Rob, who had been my pillar of strength in some areas of my life and my shield for a very long time, and all I saw was fear in a man also trying to stay strong.

The clock seemed to tick more and more loudly, and the time quickly passed as we reached that horrific moment. Finally, it was four o'clock in the morning and it was time for him to leave. As he walked to the door, he turned around and went to the kids' rooms. He hugged them in turn one more time, as I waited outside the front door.

Two of my brothers were waiting to take him to the facility which was going to be his new home for the next several years. I wrapped my arms around him with the tightest grip ever, and he held me close. Weeping uncontrollably, there were no words to describe how I felt at that moment.

A thunder-like sound of agony tore through my body as I clung to the man I had loved for fifteen years. Then he was ripped from my grasp, and in an instant, he was gone. Life as I knew it was no more. He never looked back. The car drove away leaving me standing alone outside of our home in the pre-dawn hours, sobbing hopelessly. I stood and watched as the tail lights got dimmer, and dimmer, until they faded out of sight.

After a while, I slowly walked back inside where I slumped to the floor and wrapped my arms around myself in a fetal-like position. I sobbed silently so I wouldn't wake the kids. I was confused, heartbroken, and sad, all wrapped into one. I went to the phone and dialed his number. "Please come back," I cried, "I can't do this alone." On the other end of the line he said nothing; he just listened to me cry.

"Please come back," I cried, "I can't do this alone."

†

I woke up the children at six o'clock and tried my very best to be strong. They were young, so they really needed me for almost everything. "Mom, you are not listening to me," I would hear their little voices echoing. I fought so hard to be strong—to just be a mom.

They didn't see their father that morning, but that was not unusual. Normally, in a couple of days, he would be home but not this time. Everything I believed God had told me was coming to pass; it was excruciating. And there was nothing I could do about it.

I wanted the time for them to catch the bus for school to come quickly, but it seemed like time was in slow motion. With every spare moment, I quickly went to the bathroom to dry my tears. I thought to myself that their happiness was more important than mine. Memories of their father were everywhere, and the lingering pain paralyzed me. That morning was my weakest, most helpless moment.

I must admit there were times that I was extremely angry with God for putting me through all of that. I was exhausted from crying, yet that was all I did. I was tired of being strong when the truth was that I was falling to pieces. Pretending to be strong is a challenge in and of itself. As one day piled upon another, I was thrust into reality with a busy schedule, which included his chores and mine. Some days I was so busy I did not have time to even think about my own problems.

It was baseball season and my children were all involved. I had their game practices, homework, conferences, and more on my plate, in addition to my work. I remember attending my six-year-old twins' open houses at school, each in a different classroom, at the same time. Usually, their father would go to one classroom while I attended the other. This time I was alone. I spent half the time with one child's teacher and the second half with the other's.

When I arrived at the second meeting, my eyes welled up with tears. I tried so hard to focus on what their teachers had to say, but instead I thought about Rob not being there. After the conferences concluded, I quickly left the classroom and burst into tears.

As I arrived at my car, I cried profusely in the parking lot. I knew I could not go home in the shape I found myself. My family would have fallen apart if they had seen me in that state. At home I was my family's strength. I tried diligently to make them happy; I wanted them to only see me smiling.

In the evenings, after everyone was asleep, came my crying time. I had an abundance of tears which flowed constantly. I desperately wanted to fast forward to see the ending of my pain. The unknown was killing me. I didn't know at what point in this enigmatic and tortuous story, I was going to finally be happy. It took some time for me to grasp being a single parent and then to mature to the responsibilities that lie ahead.

Even though I was ready to take hold of the situation as it was, I must say I could not have done it without my family. My brothers and their wives were always there from the beginning of Rob's legal process. My sister, even though she was thousands of miles away in England, was very supportive. My cousin, who had been a source of strength during my ordeal with Rob, was there also.

There were times I pretended to be strong, but inside I was dying. No matter how I felt, I did not withhold my pain and tears from flowing in my cousin's presence. She stood firm and constantly reminded me that God would come through. She encouraged me and said that what I was going through was a test that I must pass.

Life was an uphill battle for me because of the secret of Rob's incarceration that I was keeping from my younger children. Every day brought new challenges. My greatest challenge was my deception about their father. One day, when one of my twins started talking about Dr. Martin Luther King Jr. being in prison, I was so close to telling them the truth.

She did not know he was not a bad person. I said, "Honey, bad people are not the only ones who go to prison."

She opened her little eyes so wide and asked, "Who goes to prison, Mommy?"

That would have been the perfect opportunity for me to

tell them about their father, but instead buckets of tears welled up in my eyes and began to stream down my face. I opened my mouth to speak, but no words came out. I tried again and started to choke on my words. All three sets of eyes were staring up at me with puzzled looks on their faces. "Mommy, why are you crying?" they asked. Not to worry them any further I tried again to explain, but I simply couldn't.

My response was, "I wasn't crying. I thought she was being funny!" and I started to laugh hysterically just to prove to them I was really okay. I didn't know what was right anymore—to tell our children the truth about their father or to keep it hidden. I wondered if I was protecting them or hurting them. I really struggled to make the right decision. What will they think about him? Will they think it's all right to take the same path as he did?

They always wanted to be like their father. I have read their letters to him asking where he was. They had been searching for the truth in their letters. I had locked up the truth inside of me and I didn't know how much longer I could keep it from them.

I needed to know exactly what God wanted me to do. I already had so much with which to deal and my plate was completely full—overflowing, truth be told. It seemed like my life was in pieces. Therefore, I feared their reactions, which became another issue I had put on my plate. Even though we don't often see it, God usually prepares us for future events because what I thought was going to be horrible turned out to be tolerable.

It took a long time for me to disclose the truth. As their mother, I wanted to protect them in every way. It may not have been the right choice because they relentlessly searched for him. They all wrote letters to their father. My oldest son, about eight, was the most persistent in this endeavor; I faithfully sent the letters on to Rob.

This was another issue from which I had to release my-self. I knew it was time to tell them; I started with my oldest son. I broke the news to him with the assistance of my pas-tor. His first question was "Why?" and then, "When is he coming home?" That was all he had to say. He twiddled his thumbs and stared into space. No matter what was said to him, he would not speak and that broke my heart.

When will my heartache end? I found myself at a place where no mother ever wants to be—unable to protect her child. I excused myself from the meeting and wept. There's always something to be fixed. I knew, however, that God is trustworthy and gracious in all situations.

I am a testimony to God's grace and mercy
because He carried me and my children
through our weak and unhappy moments.

†

In your weakest moments He will carry you, even when you don't feel like you are being carried. It took approximate-ly ten months for me to grasp what was happening, to ma-ture, stand up, and face the responsibilities that were ahead. Today I am a testimony to God's grace and mercy because He carried me and my children through our weak and un-happy moments.

> *For the mind set on the flesh is death, but the mind set on the Spirit is life and peace, because the mind set on the flesh is hostile toward God; for it does not subject itself to the law of God, for it is not even able to do so, and those who are in the flesh cannot please God.*
>
> Romans 8:6-8

CHAPTER 21

Let Go and Let God

Your season of trials and tribulation is what strengthens you for God's purpose for your life. God is refining you as the smelter refines silver to obtain greater and greater purity. With each trial, He removes more dross; He refines you closer to the purity of Christ. Proverbs 25:4-5 says, "Take away the dross from the silver, and there comes out a vessel for the smith; take away the wicked before the king, and his throne will be established in righteousness." While Rob is incarcerated, he faces the consequence of frustration, loneliness, doubts, and confusion.

As I talked with Rob, I encouraged him to use his confinement to seek God for His purpose in life. When the door is opened, and he becomes a free man, his situation will change from consequence to purpose regarding his choices. When you walk in your purpose, you are constantly armed with your testimony. It's a weapon against your enemy and it reveals God's power. There is no worship without a testimony, absolutely none, because your testimony is your story of how God saved you for His glory.

Testimonies are personal. In the first instance, it is the story of how Jesus saved you for a life set apart for Him and for His glory. Added to this are our struggles and victories as we walk through this life prayerfully submitted to the Holy Spirit. They tell of awe-inspiring experiences with God. No one else has your testimony; it is personal. When you think about what the Lord has done and how He brought you through all your previous trials, you desire to rejoice in Him. Remember, when the next trial touches your life, the same God who delivered you in the past will do the same again. As you become more mature in the Lord, your trials may increase—certainly your responsibilities will.

Your deliverance from a particular situation will come with different answers: yes, no, or wait. Whatever answer God may give you, it is incumbent upon you to wait patiently for Him to move on your behalf. You can know you will be given the correct answer and will be delivered in this life or the next, even though discerning that answer may be difficult. He may answer "no," which is not a negative answer, because He knows what's best for you. If the answer is "wait" without explanation, be patient, for God's timing is perfect.

... true prosperity is the Holy Spirit living inside of you, bringing you the deep, satisfying joy of the Lord.

†

The mere fact that God answered your prayer is a blessing. When you go before Him, don't go with a preconceived mindset; always be open to His response. As a believer, you will experience this type of answer at some point in your walk with God. An extended wait can drive you to impatience, frustration, and even anger at God.

Have you ever been in a place where it seems that everyone around you is flourishing and you are not moving forward as fast as you think you should? You don't want to go to church anymore, and sometimes you stay away from people you think are thriving, while you're not. Prosperity is not always a blessing. Often it refers to material achievement, but true prosperity is the Holy Spirit living inside of you bringing you the deep, satisfying joy of the Lord.

You may assume you are blessed when everything in your life is going well and cursed when it is not. But being broken is a blessing when it matures you and increases your faith. Material prosperity is a curse if it entices you away from God. Remember the story of Lazarus and the rich man when both have died, and Lazarus was taken to the bosom of Abraham and comforted, while the rich man found himself in Hades in torment. A great chasm that could not be bridged separated them. Abraham declared to the rich man, "Child, remember that during your life you received your good things, and likewise Lazarus bad things; but now he is being comforted here, while you are in agony" (Luke 16:19-31).

If you look at your life and try to fix it yourself, you will end up at a road block. Everything must be based on trusting God completely and following His will. When the rich man asked that Lazarus be allowed to warn his five brothers, Abraham tells him that they have Moses and the prophets to warn them to repent. That is, they have the Word of God.

You must let go and let God. In Psalm 37:25 David said, "I have been young and now I am old, yet I have not seen the righteous forsaken or his descendants begging bread." Don't try to fix things on your own. There is no doubt you will end up with one conclusion: you cannot succeed. I tried for many years to sort things out myself and failed at every turn.

I had exhausted every option and came up with nothing but a dead end of frustration and misery. Only God can take you from darkness to light. Your hindrances are God's opportunity to show up and shine out in your life. In my former life, at times, I thought the way I was living was okay. I was fulfilling the lust of my flesh and my carnal mind was dictating my actions. But now I know God wants me to surrender completely to Him, and He will give me the wisdom and strength to make the corrections needed.

When Jesus starts the process of working in your life, it will create some uncomfortable situations, tears, and fears. You won't understand it all. Trust God in the good times and the bad, through the heartaches and the pain. He will never let you down because He won't give up on you.

Remember those who led you, who spoke the word of God to you; and considering the result of their conduct, imitate their faith. Jesus Christ is the same yesterday and today and forever.

Hebrews 13:7-8

If we say that we have no sin, we are deceiving ourselves and the truth is not in us. If we confess our sins, He is faithful and righteous to forigve us our sins and to cleanse us from all unrighteousness. If we say that we have not sinned, we make Him a liar and His word is not in us.

1 John 1:8-10

CHAPTER 22

Removing My Mask of Deception

I had a plan, but God had a better plan. I thought that if I covered my deception, Rob and I would eventually get married. The deception would then go away, and no one would ever know the truth. After Rob was convicted, I thought my spiritual life would fall into place, and I would no longer have the burden I had carried for so long.

I believed I was finally sanctified and holy: no more fornication, no more lies. What I didn't understand at the time is that God sees me, on one level, as pure and holy because I am justified, declared guilt-free, by Christ's sacrifice and resurrection (Romans 3:21-31). On another level, I am a work in progress as I am being sanctified, made holy (Romans 6:19; 1 Thessalonians 4:1-8), day by day by the teaching of the Holy Spirit through the study of God's word, and by communing with Him through prayer.

A confession?! Why, God?

†

A few months later the Lord told me to take off the mask, that is, make a confession. A confession?! *Why God?* I had already swept that part of my life under the rug once Rob went away. I anticipated it was time for me to move on with a clean slate, but I received the surprise of my life. Jesus called me out like He did the woman with the issue of blood (Mark 5:24-34; Luke 8:42-48; Matthew 9:19-22).

This woman, according to Jewish law (Leviticus 15:25-27), was ceremonially unclean. Anyone who touched her was likewise unclean. This woman defied the law to touch the hem of Jesus' garment. Her situation was similar to mine; we were both in a wrong place. I had no business standing before the congregation ministering to God's people, especially as Women's President, and she should not have been out in public causing others to become unclean. Jesus could have healed the woman, pretended He hadn't, and just allowed her to return quietly to her home. No one would have known she was at a place where she should not have been, but for His glory and her soul, He called her out.

He could have let my deception stay right where I had swept it—under the rug, but He was not pleased to let my sin fester any longer. One day, during a conversation with God, He impressed on me that it was time for me to confess to the congregation to which I had lied for so long. I pondered it night and day. I was afraid, but I had to obey God.

The following Sunday was Women's Sunday. I asked my pastor for permission to speak to the congregation and she granted it. After wearing the mask for so many years, it had become affixed to my face. I was going to be exposed and I wasn't sure how things were going to turn out. Standing behind the podium and ministering was always my desire and could be a joyous moment for me. While I thrived in leadership positions, because of my lifestyle, I was thoroughly unhappy. My sin enveloped me like a dark cloud. Leadership had become a tremendous burden.

As I confessed, I looked at the people in the congregation. Everyone was in shock; I could see the expressions on their faces. Some people had their hands over their mouths in disbelief. There wasn't an "amen" or "praise the Lord" echoed in the building. I sobbed at the end of my confession; I was finally free. My shame and disgrace were left at the altar, not under the rug. Before, I thought my plan of sweeping it under the rug was perfect, but the perfect plan was Jesus calling me out of the darkness of my sin and into the light of abiding in Him.

> *My shame and disgrace were left at the altar,*
> *not under the rug.*

†

What the congregation didn't realize was that I was not the only one put to the test that morning. They were also put to the test. What was going to be their reaction? Embraces, or looks of contempt? To my surprise some members embraced me, but my pastor never forgave me. I was called a liar and stripped of the position I held. I was never called in for a one-on-one meeting with my pastor, but she did tell me that I "needed to get it together."

I believed she missed the move of God because I thought I already "had it together." I agree, I lied, and I deceived the church, but that was who I was in the past. I wonder what she thinks about Jacob. Jesus pulled me up "out of the pit of destruction, out of the miry clay, and He set my feet upon a rock making my footsteps firm" (Psalm 40:2). He cleansed me with His blood (1 John 1:7), shed for me on Calvary.

130

I had to suffer the consequences of being removed as Women's President. As important as the position was to me, being free from my guilt and shame was more important. I have no regrets in that I obeyed God's call to public confession.

However, I continued to feel unclean for some time even though I had confessed and was confident the Lord had forgiven me. Why hadn't she seen me as the prodigal son's father saw him? (Luke 15:11-32) I believe what troubled me was the way the entire situation was handled pastorally, not so much that my beloved leadership position had been taken away.

My dark and gloomy story has now become a part of my testimony, not just of how the Lord Jesus saved my soul, but of how He brought me to my knees and raised me up again when I was not following in His footsteps and living in His will. He delivered me from a life of shame and disgrace. His death on the cross, His resurrection conquering death, and His ascension to glory paid for all my sin. Please focus, not on my shame and disgrace, but on my deliverance. I praise God daily for His mercy and grace.

This brings to mind the story of the woman who was caught in adultery and was brought to Jesus (John 8:1-11). Why didn't Jesus allow the scribes and Pharisees to stone the woman? Had they stoned her, He would have had to allow everyone else to be stoned. Were they without sin? Jesus gave them permission to stone her, only if they were themselves sinless.

Their sin didn't allow them to stone her because no one was found sinless, except for Jesus, who has the ultimate authority to condemn anyone. Instead, He lovingly gave the woman an opportunity to start all over and walk with Him.

Has God offered you the same opportunity that He gave the adulterous woman? What will you do with this opportunity? As for me, I have been set free. You, Lord, paid the price for my sins and I am forever grateful. Thank You for my freedom from bondage.

You, Lord, paid the price for my sins and I am forever grateful.

†

> *Our Father which art in heaven, Hallowed be thy name. Thy kingdom come. Thy will be done in earth, as it is in heaven. Give us this day our daily bread. And forgive us our debts, as we forgive our debtors. And lead us not into temptation, but deliver us from evil: For thine is the kingdom, and the power, and the glory, for ever. Amen.*
>
> Matthew 6:9-13 KJV

CHAPTER 23

Never Again

With my deliverance from my many years out of the will of God regarding my life with Rob, I am determined that never again will I suffer physical or verbal abuse. I am resolute that I will live in the will of my Lord, by the power of the Holy Spirit, so as to avoid as many of the consequences of sin as is humanly possible. I am living with enough of the consequences of my actions for a lifetime.

I have gained my independence and I enjoy being free. I am like a bird flying in the sky. I can boldly say this because I know God chose my beloved husband. He is heaven sent. He loves and respects me completely, as I do him.

I know God chose my beloved husband. He is heaven sent.

†

The more the Lord directed my steps, the more I realized He had taken Rob out of my life as my partner. I know he is the father of my three youngest children and I will always care for him and do whatever I can to help him. But at this point of my life, God has closed that chapter and I've completely accepted it.

I'd like to add a word about Xaria's father Mitch. He is a wonderful man who did not deserve what I did to him in breaking off our relationship for the love of security and wealth that I believed Rob could offer us. He maintains a wonderful relationship with our daughter and for that I am forever grateful.

Now, a new chapter has been opened in my life, and the missing pieces of the puzzle have finally been put into place. I fought against the riptide for a very long time. During high winds, when the wind is blowing at an angle to the beach, there comes a critical point when the water rushes out from the beach and is swiftly swept out and into the deep sea. Only if you know to swim parallel to the beach before swimming to land, do you escape being taken out to sea and drowned.

I was caught in the riptide of my sin and had forgotten the most basic rule of God's will—obedience to His Word. While I loved Him and sought to serve Him, and in fact did serve Him in some ways, I turned a blind eye to His instructions on sexual purity. I lived with a man who was not my husband and had three beautiful children with him. This godly instruction I should have clearly understood and obeyed, but I did not.

I was caught in the riptide of my sin.

†

I could blame the culture in which I live, a culture which thinks nothing of living with a person who is not one's spouse, and even having children with them outside of the bonds of marriage. Yet I was at fault, trapped in my own sinful, carnal desires of wealth, security, and relationship. I am

134

grateful that the Lord rescued me from my own foolishness before being drowned by my sin.

Even Christians say, what does it really matter that a man and a woman have sexual relations outside of marriage, the most intimate of human relationships? The Bible pictures Christ as the bridegroom awaiting His bride, the church,[3] pure and undefiled. Covenantal marriage is God's expression of His perfect love, and as such it is His protection for His people. Rightly understood, it is a covenant, a contract, between the man, the woman, and God. Biblical marriage is a testimony of God's provision and grace to all as God's plan for our lives, which runs counter to the society in which we live. Sexual relationships only within marriage prevent many of the most egregious ills in the church and in greater society.

*Now, with full conviction, my past is buried
and my future resurrected.*

†

It took the closing of the previous chapter in my life and the opening of this new one for me to conclude that "God causes all things to work together for good to those who love God, to those who are called according to His purpose" (Romans 8:28). God, who is omniscient, all-knowing, knows Rob has some very good qualities, but they were not enough for where God is taking me. Rob and I were like two ships passing in the night. I am grateful for the heartache and pain for I have seen God work mightily in my life because of the depths to which I had fallen. The gift is truly in the pain.

---

3   The true church is the "body of Christ [which] began on the day of Pentecost.... It was founded upon the death, resurrection and ascension of Christ and such an accomplished fact was not possible until Pentecost (Gal. 3:23-25).... [T]he Holy Spirit, Who came at Pentecost, arrived to perform among His various ministries of regeneration, sealing, indwelling and filling, His distinctive ministry for this age, of baptizing into Christ, that is, into His body the church (I Cor. 12:13)." (Unger, Merrill F., *Unger's Bible Dictionary*, Third Edition, Chicago, Moody Press, 1976)

My life now is nothing like what it was in my past. I don't blame Rob because I, too, made a plethora of mistakes. In fact, I didn't just make mistakes, I accepted much sin in my life and clung to it like a life preserver. The life preserver did not serve to bring me to the shore of God's will. I was caught in a riptide which was taking me farther and farther out to sea.

I entered a relationship in which I should never have been, but once in, believed I was too deeply ensconced to get out. Having the wrong motive—security in a man—kept me out of the will of God. Now, with full conviction, my past is buried and my future resurrected. In life, I believe God will make every attempt to separate you from people and things which do not fit into His grand plans. Moving forward with God requires unity with Him. To have one person pulling one way and the other pulling the opposite way will never achieve the mighty move of God in your life.

I am confident that Rob, though at times supportive of me, would not have permitted me to do what God instructed because of his lack of understanding, and constant need to be in control. I'm joyful and grateful that this new season of my life does not include abuse of any kind, subtle or not so subtle.

Life is a journey. With every step I take, I gain wisdom whether I succeed or fail in an endeavor. God has done a new work in my life, and I cherish it. My advice to you is this: don't fight against the will of God because the result of being in His will always bring deep satisfaction and beauty in the end. And I pray you will say as our Lord Jesus Christ taught us, "Thy kingdom come, Thy will be done, in earth as it is in heaven" (Matthew 6:10).

Amen.

†

Epilogue

A few years have passed since I initially penned my story. For a time, I lived the life of a single mom of four that I had dreaded all those years. When I met my husband Clive, I had created a nearly impenetrable, high barrier around my heart because I was determined that I would never again let another man hurt me the way Rob had. I felt certain that I would never love again, fearing that I might again be deeply wounded.

Time spent with Clive proved to me that not all men are cut from the same cloth, any more than are all women. I began to feel safe, to put my guard down. I found myself very much in love and willing to make a covenant with him before our God. We were married about two years ago in an intimate ceremony in South Florida.

At times, I still forget that in all marriages spouses have differing points of view and therefore disagreements. Whenever our marriage encounters a dispute, I can be quick to smell a rat, to be suspicious, and quickly be on guard, busily erecting walls.

Clive has been patient with me as my barrier building has become less frequent and less fortified. He continues to be calm and patient. He once told me that it is remarkably challenging to be married to a woman who is broken, even though I am in the process of healing by the grace of God.

Before we married, he asked me this question, "If I give you my heart, will you please promise never to break it?" I pledged to do so, and I take this vow seriously, as unto my Lord.

With Rob still in prison, Clive has stepped in as a father to my children. The sound of laughter often fills our home, loudly proclaiming that he is playing with the kids. The evening falls into a studious silence as he helps them with their homework. Like any engaged, worthy father, he reprimands them when deserved, all the while reminding them that he loves them. Clive attends every school conference and signs off on homework. I am truly grateful for his steady, committed presence in our lives as both husband to me and father to my children.

As for my children, they are all doing well. Xaria lives and works at our family business in South Florida. Dante, Jayden, and Jayda attend public school in Central Florida.

My Mom continues to live with us and is a tremendous blessing to our family. She graciously helps the children, Clive, and me, for which I am eternally grateful. We could not have accomplished all that we have without her stable presence, encouragement, and love.

Our Lord and time have largely healed me, and I have learned that my marriage relationship is far removed from the abuse that I've experienced in my life, often with my complicity, I might add. I am now pleased and gratified to see my husband happy, as well as the fact that we are enjoying a healthier and very loving marriage.

There is more to my story and to Clive's. If you'd like to keep abreast of what we are doing in our lives and ministry, you may contact us on our website: TheDivineMoment.com. If you would like to sample the two CDs for which I have written lyrics, you'll find them on our website, along with other projects we are undertaking. May the Lord use my story to His glory.

Georgette Crandall Foster
October 2018

The Divine Moment Ministry
Clive and Georgette Crandall Foster
TheDivineMoment.com